THE CONSOLATIONS OF THE FOREST

THE
CONSOLATIONS
OF THE
FOREST

✿✿

**ALONE IN A CABIN
ON THE SIBERIAN TAIGA**

SYLVAIN TESSON

Translated from the French by Linda Coverdale

Rizzoli
ex libris

First published in the United States of America in 2013
By Rizzoli Ex Libris, an imprint of
Rizzoli International Publications, Inc.
300 Park Avenue South
New York, NY 10010
www.rizzoliusa.com

Originally published in France as *Dans les Forêts de Sibérie*
Copyright © Editions Gallimard, Paris, 2011
Translation Copyright © 2013 Linda Coverdale

2013 2014 2015 2016 / 10 9 8 7 6 5 4 3 2 1

Distributed in the U.S. trade by Random House, New York
Printed in U.S.A.

ISBN-13: 978-0-8478-4127-1

Library of Congress Catalog Control Number: 2013931305

To Arnaud Humann

For I belong to the forests and solitude.

—KNUT HAMSUN, *Pan*

Freedom is always available. One need only pay the price for it.

—HENRY DE MONTHERLANT, *Cahiers, 1957*

CONTENTS

A SIDESTEP

I'D PROMISED MYSELF that before I turned forty I would live as a hermit deep in the woods.

I went to spend six months in a Siberian cabin on the shores of Lake Baikal, on the tip of North Cedar Cape. Seventy-five miles from the nearest village, no neighbors, no access roads, and every now and then, a visit. Wintertime temperatures in the minus twenties Fahrenheit; the summer brought bears out into the open. In short: paradise.

I took along books, cigars, and vodka. The rest—space, silence, and solitude—was already there.

In that desert, I created a beautiful and temperate life for myself, experiencing an existence centered on simple gestures. Between the lake and the forest, I watched the days go by. I cut wood, fished for my dinner, read a lot, hiked in the

1

mountains, and drank vodka, at my window. The cabin was an ideal observation post from which to witness nature's every move.

I knew winter and spring, happiness, despair, and in the end, peace.

In the depths of the taiga, I changed myself completely. Staying put brought me what I could no longer find on any journey. The genius loci helped me to tame time. My hermitage became the laboratory of these transformations.

Every day I recorded my thoughts in a notebook.

This is the journal of a hermit's life.

S. T.

✿✿✿✿✿✿✿✿✿✿✿✿✿✿✿✿✿✿✿✿✿✿✿✿✿✿✿✿✿✿✿✿✿✿✿✿✿✿✿

The Forest

THE HEINZ COMPANY sells around fifteen kinds of tomato sauce. The supermarket in Irkutsk stocks them all and I don't know which to choose. I've already filled six carts with dried pasta and Tabasco. The blue truck is waiting for me; it's –26° F outside, and Misha, the driver, keeps the engine running. Tomorrow we leave Irkutsk and in three days will reach the cabin, on the western shore of the lake. I must finish my shopping today. I decide on Heinz Super Hot Tapas. I buy eighteen bottles: three per month.

Fifteen kinds of ketchup. That's the sort of thing that made me want to withdraw from this world.

FEBRUARY 9

I'm stretched out on my bed in Nina's house on Proletariat Street. I like Russian street names. In the villages you'll find a Labor Street, an October Revolution Street, a Partisans Street, and sometimes an Enthusiasm Street, along which trudge gray-haired Slav grannies.

Nina is the best landlady in Irkutsk. A former pianist, she used to play in the concert halls of the Soviet Union. Now she runs a guest house. Yesterday she told me, "Who'd ever have thought I'd wind up cranking out pancakes?" Nina's cat is purring on my stomach. If I were a cat, I know whose tummy I'd snuggle on.

I'm poised on the threshold of a seven-year-old dream. In 2003 I stayed for the first time at Lake Baikal. Walking along the shore, I discovered cabins at regular intervals, inhabited by strangely happy recluses. The idea of going to ground alone in the forest, surrounded by silence, began to intrigue me. Seven years later, here I am.

I must find the strength to push the cat off. Getting up from a bed requires amazing energy. Especially when it's to change a life. This longing to retreat just at the point of achieving your heart's desire. . . . Certain men do an about-face at the crucial moment. I'm afraid I might be one of them.

Misha's truck is packed to the point of bursting. It's a five-hour drive to the lake across frozen steppes, navigating over petrified wave crests and troughs. Villages smoke at the foot of hills, wreathed in mists trapped in the shallows. Faced with visions like these, the Suprematist painter Kazimir Malevich wrote, "Whoever has crossed Siberia can never again aspire to happiness." At the top of a ridge, there it is: the lake. We stop to have a drink. After four brimming glasses of vodka, we wonder: *How in the world does the shoreline manage to follow the water so perfectly?*

Let's get the statistics out of the way. Baikal: 435 miles long, 50 miles wide, almost a mile deep. Twenty-five million years old. The winter ice is over three and a half feet thick. Beaming its love down upon the white surface, the sun doesn't give a damn about such things. Filtered by clouds, patches of sunshine slide in a gleaming herd across the snow, brightening its cadaverous cheeks.

The truck ventures out onto the ice. Beneath the wheels, it's two thirds of a mile down. If the truck plunges through a fissure, it will descend into a black abyss. The bodies will sink in silence. Slow snowfall of the drowned. The lake is a godsend for anyone who dreads decay. James Dean wanted to die and leave "a beautiful corpse." The tiny copepods called *Epischura baikalensis* will clean the bodies within twenty-four hours, leaving only ivory bones on the lake bed.[1]

FEBRUARY 10

We spent the night in the village of Khuzhir on Olkhon Island, pronounced "Olkrhone," Nordic style, and we're heading north. Misha isn't a talker. I admire people who keep quiet; I imagine their thoughts.

I'm on my way to the place of my dreams. Outside, the atmosphere is bleak. The cold has let its hair down in the wind; wisps of snow skitter away from our wheels. The storm wedges itself into the cleft between sky and ice. I study the shore, trying not to think about living for six months in the requiem mass of those forests. All the ingredients of the imagery of Siberian deportation are there: the vastness, the livid cast of the light. The ice rather resembles a shroud. Innocent people were dumped for twenty-five years into this nightmare, whereas I will be living here by choice. Why should I complain?

Misha: "It's dreary."

And nothing more until the next day.

Constructed in the 1980s as a geologist's hut, my cabin is off in a clearing of the cedar forest in the northern sector of the Baikal-Lena Nature Preserve. My new neighborhood is named after these trees: North Cedar Cape. It sounds like an old-people's home. And after all, I am going on a retreat.

Driving on a lake is a transgression. Only gods and spiders walk on water. Three times in my life I've felt I was breaking a taboo. The first was when I contemplated the dry bed of the once-mighty Aral Sea, emptied by Man. The second was when I read a woman's private diary. The third was driving over the waters of Baikal. Each time, the feeling of tearing aside a veil. The eye spying through the keyhole.

I explain this to Misha. And get no reply.

Tonight we stay at the weather station of Pokoyniki, in the heart of the preserve.

Sergei and Natasha run the station. They're as beautiful as Greek gods, but wearing more clothes. They've been living here for twenty years, tracking down poachers. My cabin is thirty-one miles to the north of their home, and I'm glad to have them as neighbors. I'll find pleasure in thinking about them. Their love: an island in the Siberian winter.

We spend the evening with two of their friends, Sasha and Yura, Siberian fishermen who embody two Dostoyevskian character types. Sasha is hypertensive, with a florid face, full of vitality. He has the eyes of a Mongol, and a deep, steely gaze. Yura is somber, Rasputinian, an eater of bottom-feeding fish. He's as pale as the denizens of Tolkien's Mordor. Sasha is made for great feats, impulsive action, while Yura is a born conspirator. He hasn't set foot in a city in fifteen years.

FEBRUARY 11

In the morning we take to the ice again. The forest streams past. When I was twelve, my family went to see the Mémorial de Verdun, a museum dedicated to the Great War. I remember the Chemin des Dames hall, commemorating a trench where soldiers and their rifles had been engulfed by a flood of mud. The forest this morning is a buried army, of which nothing shows but its bayonets.

The ice cracks. Sheets compressed by movement in the mantle explode; fault lines streak across the quicksilver plain, spewing crystalline chaos. Blue blood flows from wounded glass.

"It's lovely," says Misha.

And nothing else until that evening.

At seven p.m. my cape appears. North Cedar Cape. My cabin. The GPS coordinates are: N 54°26'45.12"/E 108° 32'40.32".

The small dark forms of some people with dogs are advancing along the shore to welcome us. That's how Breughel painted country folk. Winter transforms everything into a Dutch tableau, glossy and precise.

Snow falls, and then night, and all this white turns a dreadful black.

FEBRUARY 12

Volodya T., a fifty-year-old forest ranger, has lived with his wife, Ludmila, in the cabin on North Cedar Cape for fifteen years. He has a gentle face and wears dark glasses. Some Russians look like brutes; Volodya would care tenderly for a bear cub. He and Ludmila want to move back to Irkutsk. Ludmila has phlebitis and needs medical attention. Like all Russian women steeped in tea, Ludmila has skin that is frog-belly white, and her veins look like vermicelli beneath its pearly luster. Now that I have arrived, the ranger and his wife will leave.

The cabin smokes in its grove of cedars. Snow has meringued the roof, and the beams are the color of gingerbread. I'm hungry.

With its back to the mountains, the cabin nestles at the bottom of slopes 6,500 feet high. Coniferous taiga rises toward the summits, giving up at about 3,300 feet. Beyond lies the realm of ice, stone, and sky. From my windows I can see the shores of the lake, which lies at an elevation of almost 1,500 feet.

Spaced about nineteen miles apart, the preserve's stations are manned by rangers under Sergei's command. To the north, on Cape Elohin, my neighbor's name is Volodya. To the south, in the hamlet of Zavorotni, another one, Volodya E. Later on, melancholy and in want of a drinking companion, I'll need simply to trudge north for five hours or south for one day.

Sergei, the head ranger, came with us from Pokoyniki. We clambered out of the truck and surveyed the splendor before us in silence. Then, touching his temple, Sergei announced: "This is a stupendous place to commit suicide." A friend of mine, Arnaud, has also come along in the truck with me from Irkutsk, where he has been living for the past fifteen years. He married the most beautiful woman in the city, who'd been dreaming of Cannes and the Avenue Montaigne. When she realized that Arnaud thought only of running around the taiga, she left him.

For the next few days, we'll all get me set up in my cabin. Then my friends will go home, leaving me alone. Task at hand: unloading the truck.

**REQUISITE SUPPLIES FOR SIX
MONTHS IN THE BOREAL FOREST**
Ax and cleaver
Tarp
Burlap bag
Pickax
Dip net

Ice skates

Snowshoes

Kayak and paddle

Fishing poles, line, weights

Fly-fishing flies and spoons

Kitchen utensils

Teapot

Ice drill

Rope

Dagger and Swiss Army knife

Whetstone

Kerosene lamp

Kerosene

Candles

GPS, compass, map

Solar panels, cables, and rechargeable batteries

Matches and lighters

Mountain backpacks

Duffel bags

Felt carpet

Sleeping bags

Mountaineering equipment

Mosquito-net face mask

Gloves

Felt boots

Ice ax

Crampons

Pharmaceuticals (10 boxes of acetaminophen for vodka
      hangovers)

Saw

Hammer, nails, screws, file

French flag for Bastille Day
Hand-launched anti-bear flares
Flare gun
Rain cape
Outdoor grill
Folding saw
Tent
Ground cloth
Headlamp
−40° F sleeping bag
Royal Canadian Mounted Police jacket
Plastic luge
Boots with gaiters
Liquor glasses and vodka
90% alcohol to make up for any shortage of the above article
Personal library
Cigars, cigarillos, incense paper, and a Tupperware container
    "humidor"
Icons (Saint Seraphim of Sarov, Saint Nicholas, the imperial
    family of the last Romanovs, Tsar Nicholas II, black
    Virgin)
Wooden trunks
Binoculars
Electronic appliances
Pens and notebooks
Provisions (six-month supply of pasta, rice, Tabasco,
    hardtack, canned fruit, red and black pepper, salt,
    coffee, honey, and tea)

It's funny: you decide to live in a cabin, and envision yourself smoking a cigar under the open sky, lost in meditation . . .

and you wind up checking off items on supply lists like an army quartermaster. Life comes down to grocery shopping.

I push open the door of the cabin. In Russia, Formica reigns supreme. Seventy years of historical materialism have obliterated the Russian sense of aesthetics. Where does bad taste come from? Why use linoleum at all? How did kitsch take over the world? The principal phenomenon of globalization has been a worldwide embrace of the ugly. If you need convincing, just walk around a Chinese village, check out the latest decor in French post offices, or consider what tourists wear. Bad taste is the common denominator of humanity.

For two days, with Arnaud's help, I tear off the linoleum, oilcloth, polyester tarp material, and adhesive plastic papers that cover the walls. We crowbar our way through cardboard panels. Stripped clean, the interior reveals logs pearled with resin and a pale yellow wood floor, like that of Van Gogh's room in Arles. Volodya watches us in consternation. He does not *see* that the bare, amber-colored wood is more beautiful to the eye than oilcloth. He listens as I explain this to him. I am the bourgeois defending the superiority of a parquet floor over linoleum. Aestheticism is a form of reactionary deviance.

We have brought two yellow pine double-paned windows from Irkutsk to replace the cabin windows, which shed a dreary light. Sergei enlarges the embrasures by cutting the logs with a chainsaw, working hectically, nonstop, without calculating the angles, correcting the mistakes he makes in his haste as he goes along. Russians always build things with a sense of urgency, as if fascist soldiers were going to pour over the hill at any minute.

In the villages sprinkled around this territory, Russians feel the fragility of their position. That little nursery-tale pig in his house of straw was about as vulnerable. Living within four wooden walls amid frozen marshes calls for modest ambitions, and these hamlets are not made to last. They're a clutch of shacks creaking in the north wind. The Romans built for the ages; a Russian just wants to get through the winter.

Given the violence of the storms, the cabin is a matchbox. A creature of the forest, destined to rot; the trunks of the clearing's trees furnished the logs for its walls. The cabin will return to the soil when abandoned by its owner, yet in its simplicity it offers perfect protection against the seasonal cold without disfiguring the sheltering forest. With the yurt and the igloo, it figures among the handsomest human responses to environmental adversity.

FEBRUARY 13

Ten more hours spent ridding the clearing of trash, sprucing the place up to lure back the genius loci. Russians make a clean sweep of the past, but not of their refuse. Throw something away? *I'd rather die*, they say. Why toss out a tractor engine when the piston might make a good lamp base? The territory of the former Soviet Union is littered with the crud of Five-Year Plans: factories in ruins, machine tools, the carcasses of planes. Many Russians live in places that resemble construction sites and auto junkyards. They do *not* see refuse, mentally ignoring the spectacle before them. When you live on a dump, you need to know how to edit things out.

FEBRUARY 14

The last crate contains books. If asked why I've come to shut myself up here, I'll say I was behind in my reading. I nail a pine plank up over my bedstead to hold my books. I've got at least seventy. Back in Paris I took pains to put together an ideal list. When you have misgivings about the poverty of your inner life, it's important to bring along good books to fill that void in a pinch. The mistake would be to choose only difficult reading on the assumption that life in the woods would keep your spiritual temperature at a fever pitch, but time drags on when all you've got for snowy afternoons is Hegel.

Before I left, a friend advised me to take along the *Memoirs* of Cardinal de Retz, a classic of seventeenth-century French literature, and Paul Morand's biography of Nicolas Fouquet, the ill-starred Superintendant of Finances under Louis XIV. I already knew that one must never travel with books related to one's destination; in Venice, read Lermontov, but at Baikal, Byron.

I empty the crate. I have the novelists Michel Tournier for daydreaming, Michel Déon for melancholy, D. H. Lawrence for sensuality, and Yukio Mishima for steely coldness. I have a small collection of books on life in the woods: Grey Owl for his radical stance, Daniel Defoe for myth, Aldo Leopold for ethics, and Thoreau for philosophy, although I find his sermonizing a touch wearing. Whitman—he's enchanting: his *Leaves of Grass* is a work of grace. Ernst Jünger invented the expression "recourse to the forest"; I have four or five of his books. A little poetry and some philosophers as well: Nietzsche, Schopenhauer, the Stoics. Sade and Casanova to stir up my blood. Some crime fiction, because sometimes you need a breather. A few nature guides for birds, plants, and insects published by Delachaux and Niestlé. When you invite yourself into the woods, the least you can do is know the names of your hosts; indifference would be an affront. If some people were to install themselves in my apartment by force, I should at least like them to call me by my first name. The section of my Pléiade volumes in their glossy covers gleams in the candlelight. My books are icons. For the first time in my life, I'm going to read a novel straight through.

LIST OF IDEAL READING MATERIAL CAREFULLY COMPOSED IN PARIS FOR A SIX-MONTH STAY IN THE SIBERIAN FOREST

Hell Quay, Ingrid Astier

Lady Chatterley's Lover, D. H. Lawrence

The Sickness unto Death, Kierkegaard

Tales of a Lost Kingdom: A Journey into Northwest Pakistan, Erik L'Homme

Un théâtre qui marche [An Itinerant Theater], Philippe Fenwick

Lost in the Taiga: One Russian Family's Fifty-Year Struggle for Survival and Religious Freedom in the Siberian Wilderness, Vasily Peskov

Indian Creek Chronicles: A Winter Alone in the Wilderness, Pete Fromm

Men Possessed by God: The Story of the Desert Monks of Ancient Christendom, Jacques Lacarrière

Friday; or, The Other Island, Michel Tournier

Un taxi mauve, Michel Déon

Philosophy in the Boudoir, Sade

Gilles, Drieu la Rochelle

Robinson Crusoe, Daniel Defoe

In Cold Blood, Truman Capote

Un an de cabane [A Year in a Cabin in the Yukon], Olaf
    Candau

Nuptials [second collection of essays], Camus

The Fall, Camus

An Island to Oneself, Tom Neale

The Reveries of the Solitary Walker, Rousseau

The Story of My Life, Casanova

The Song of the World, Giono

Fouquet, Paul Morand

Carnets [Notebooks], Montherlant

Journal vol. 1, 1965–1970, Jünger

The Rebel's Treatise; or, Back to the Forest, Jünger

The Gordian Knot, Jünger

Approaches, Drugs, and Intoxication, Jünger

African Games, Jünger

The Flowers of Evil, Baudelaire

The Postman Always Rings Twice, James M. Cain

The Poet, Michael Connelly

Blood on the Moon, James Ellroy

Eve, James Hadley Chase

The Stoics, Pléiade edition

Red Harvest, Dashiell Hammett

On the Nature of Things, Lucretius

The Myth of the Eternal Return: Cosmos and History, Mircea
    Eliade

The World as Will and Representation, Schopenhauer

Typhoon, Conrad

Odes, Victor Segalen

Life of Rancé, Chateaubriand

Tao Te Ching, Lao Tzu

The Marienbad Elegy, Goethe
The Complete Novels, Hemingway
Ecce Homo, Nietzsche
Thus Spake Zarathustra, Nietzsche
Twilight of the Idols, or, How to Philosophize with a Hammer,
    Nietzsche
*The Stars, the Snow, the Fire: Twenty-five Years in the Alaska
    Wilderness*, John Haines
The Men of the Last Frontier, Grey Owl
Traité de la cabane solitaire [*Treatise on Solitary Cabins*],
    Antoine Marcel
At the Heart of the World, Blaise Cendrars
Leaves of Grass, Whitman
A Sand County Almanac, Aldo Leopold
The Abyss; or, Zeno of Bruges, Marguerite Yourcenar
The Thousand and One Nights
A Midsummer Night's Dream, Shakespeare
The Merry Wives of Windsor, Shakespeare
Twelfth Night; or, What You Will, Shakespeare
Arthurian Romances, Chrétien de Troyes
American Black Box, Maurice G. Dantec
American Psycho, Bret Easton Ellis
Walden, Thoreau
The Unbearable Lightness of Being, Milan Kundera
The Temple of the Golden Pavilion, Yukio Mishima
Promise at Dawn, Romain Gary
Out of Africa, Karen Blixen
The Adventurers, José Giovanni

Six days after I left Irkutsk, my friends vanish over the horizon in the blue truck. No sight is more poignant to a castaway than the disappearance of a ship's sail. Volodya and

Ludmila are off to Irkutsk and their new life. I wait for the moment when they'll turn around for a last look at the cabin.

They don't turn around.

The truck dwindles to a dot. I am alone. The mountains seem harsher now. Intense, the landscape reveals itself. The land is *in my face*. It's incredible how much mankind hogs its own attention. The presence of others makes the world fade out. Solitude is this reconquest of the enjoyment of things.

It's −27° F. The truck has dissolved into the fog. Silence falls from the sky in little white shavings. To be alone is to hear silence. A blast of wind; sleet muddles the view. I let out a scream. I open my arms, raise my face to the icy emptiness, and go back inside where it's warm.

I'm poised on the gangway.

I will finally find out if I have an inner life.

FEBRUARY 15

My first evening on my own. In the beginning, I don't dare move around much, anesthetized by the perspective of the days ahead. At ten o'clock, explosions shatter the stillness; the air has warmed up to 10° F, and the sky looks like snow. The cabin couldn't shake any harder if Russian artillery were pounding the lake. I step outside into the mild flakes to listen to the staggering blows. Currents are heaving at the lake ice.

Imprisoned, the water pleads for release. Setting a screen between life and the stars, the ice separates creatures from the sky: fish, seaweeds, micro-organisms, marine mammals, arthropods.

The cabin measures ten feet by ten feet. Heat is supplied by a cast-iron stove, which will become my friend. I put up with the snoring of this particular companion. The stove is the axis of the world, around which everything is organized. It's a little god with its own life, and when I offer it wood, I honor *Homo erectus*, who mastered fire. In his *Psychoanalysis of Fire*, Gaston Bachelard imagines that the idea of rubbing two sticks to kindle a spark was inspired by the frictions of love. While fucking, man intuited the creation of fire. Nice to know. To dampen the libido, remember to stare at dying embers.

I have two windows. One looks southward, the other to the east. Through the latter I see, some sixty miles away, the snowy crests of Buryatia, an autonomous republic within the Russian Federation, while through the other window I can trace, behind the branches of a fallen pine, the line of the bay as it curves away to the south.

My table, set right up against the eastern window, occupies its entire width, in the Russian fashion. Slavs can sit for hours watching raindrops on windowpanes. Once in a while they get up, invade a country, have a revolution, and then go back to dreaming at their windows in overheated rooms. In the winter they sip tea interminably, in no hurry to go outside.

FEBRUARY 16

At noon, outdoors.

The sky has powdered the taiga, shaking velvety down over the *vert-de-bronze* of the cedars. Winter forest: a silvery fur tossed onto the shoulders of the terrain. Waves of vegetation cover the slopes. This desire of the trees to invade everything. The forest, an ocean swell in slow motion. At every fold in the relief, black streaks darken the egg-white crowns of the trees.

How can people adore abstract fancies more than the beauty of snow crystals?

FEBRUARY 17

This morning the sun hoisted itself over the peaks of Buryatia at 8:17. A sunbeam came through the window, striking the logs of the cabin. I was in my sleeping bag. I thought the wood was bleeding.

The last flickers in the stove die at around four a.m., and by dawn, the room is freezing. I have to rise and light the fire: two actions that celebrate the passage from hominid to man. I begin my day by blowing on embers, after which I go back to bed until the cabin has reached the temperature of a new-laid egg.

This morning I grease the weapon Sergei left with me, a signal flare pistol like the one used by sailors in distress. The barrel launches a blinding charge of phosphorus to squelch the ardors of a bear or an intruder.

I have no gun and will not be hunting. To begin with, hunting is not allowed in the nature preserve. Second, I would consider it a dirty trick to shoot down the living creatures of these woods in which I am a guest. Do you like it when strangers attack you? It doesn't bother me that creatures more noble, better made, and far more muscular than I roam freely in the open forest.

This place isn't the Forêt de Chantilly. When poachers run into the gamekeepers, guns are drawn. Sergei never patrols without his rifle. Along the shores of the lake lie tombs bearing the names of rangers: a simple cement stele decorated with plastic flowers and, every so often, the guy's photo engraved on a metal medallion. As for the poachers, they have no graves.

I think about what happens to minks. Being born in the forest, surviving the winters, falling into a trap—and winding up as a coat for old hags who wouldn't last three minutes out in the taiga. If at least they were as graceful as the mustelids that are skinned for them ... Sergei told me a story. The governor of the Irkutsk region was hunting bears from his helicopter in the mountains overlooking Baikal. Destabilized by the wind, the M18 crashed. *Tableau de chasse*: eight dead. Sergei: "The bears must have danced a polka around the bonfire."

My other weapon is a dagger made in Chechnya, a handsome knife with a wooden handle, which never leaves my side all day. In the evening, I stick it into the beam over my bed. Deeply enough so that it doesn't fall down while I'm dreaming and slice open my belly.

FEBRUARY 18

I wanted to settle an old score with time. I had discovered that walking provided a way to slow it down. The alchemy of travel thickens seconds: those spent on the road passed less quickly than the others. Frantic with restlessness, I required fresh horizons and conceived a passionate interest in airports, where everything is an invitation to departure. I dreamed of ending up in a terminal. My trips began as escapes and finished in track races against the hours.

Two years ago, I chanced to spend three days in a tiny *izba*, a traditional Russian log cabin. A ranger, Anton, had welcomed me into his home on the eastern shore of Lake Baikal. Anton was so farsighted that behind his glasses, his goggle-eyes gave him the look of a gleeful toad. At night we played chess, and during the day I helped him haul in the nets. We spoke hardly at all but we read a lot: for me, the "decadent" nineteenth-century novelist Huysmans, and for him, Hemingway (which he pronounced Rhaymingvayee). He sloshed down gallons of tea; I went walking in the woods. Sunlight flooded the room. Geese were fleeing the autumn, and I thought about my dear ones. We listened to the radio. Whenever the female announcer reported the temperatures in Sochi, Anton would say: "It must be nice, down at the Black Sea." From time to time he'd toss a log into the stove, and at day's end, he'd get out the chessboard. We'd sip at some Siberian vodka from Krasnoyarsk and push the pawns around: I was always white and often lost. The endless days passed quickly, and when I left my friend, I thought, "This is the life for me." All I had to do was ask of immobility what travel no longer brought me: peace.

That was when I promised myself I would live alone in a cabin for a few months. Cold, silence, and solitude are conditions that tomorrow will become more valuable than gold. On an overpopulated, overheated, and noisy planet, a forest cabin is an El Dorado. Over nine hundred miles to the south, China is humming with a billion and a half human beings, running out of water, wood, and space. Living in the forest next to the world's largest reserve of fresh water is a luxury. One day, the Saudi oilmen, the Indian nouveaux riches, and the Russian businessmen who drag their ennui around the marble lobbies of palaces will understand this. Then it will be time to go a step up in latitude to the tundra. Happiness will lie beyond the 60th parallel north.

Better to live joyfully in a wilderness clearing than languish in a city. In the sixth volume of *The Earth and Its Inhabitants*, the geographer Élysée Reclus—a master anarchist and antiquated stylist—proposes a superb idea. The future of humanity would lie in "the complete union of the civilized with the savage." There would be no need to choose between our hunger for technological progress and our thirst for unspoiled places. Life in the forest offers an ideal terrain for this reconciliation between the archaic and the futuristic. An eternal existence unfolds beneath the treetops, literally at one with the earth. There we can reconnect with the truth of moonlit nights, submitting to the doctrine of the forests without renouncing the benefits of modernity. My cabin shelters the happy union of progress and the past. Before I came here, I selected from the department store of civilization a few products indispensable to happiness—books, cigars, vodka—and I will enjoy them in the rugged surroundings of the woods. I followed the intuitions of Reclus so faithfully that I've equipped my home with solar panels, which run a small computer. The silicon of my integrated circuits feeds on photons. I listen to Schubert while watching the snow, I read Marcus Aurelius after my wood-chopping chores, I smoke a Havana to celebrate the evening's fishing. Reclus would be pleased.

In *What Am I Doing Here?* Bruce Chatwin quotes Jünger quoting Stendhal: "The art of civilization consists in combining the most delicate pleasures with the constant presence of danger." An observation that echoes Élysée's injunction. The essential thing is to live one's life with a brave hand on the tiller, swinging boldly between contrasting worlds. Balancing between danger and pleasure, the frigid Russian winter and the warmth of a stove. Never settling, always oscillating from one to the other extremity on the spectrum of sensations.

*

Life in the woods allows us to pay our debts. We breathe, eat fruit, pick flowers; we bathe in a river's waters, and then one day we die without paying the bill to the planet. Life is sneaking a meal in a restaurant. The ideal would be to go through life like the Scandinavian troll who roams the moorland without leaving any tracks in the heather. Robert Baden-Powell's advice should be made a universal principle: "When through with a campsite, take care to leave two things behind. Firstly: nothing. Secondly: your thanks." What is essential? Not to weigh too heavily on the surface of the globe. Shut inside his cube of logs, the hermit does not soil the Earth. From the threshold of his *izba*, he watches the seasons perform the dance of the eternal return. Possessing no machines, he keeps his body fit. Cut off from all communication, he deciphers the language of the trees. Released from the grip of television, he discovers that a window is more transparent than a TV screen. His cabin provides comfort and brightens up the lakeshore. One day, we tire of talking about "de-growth" and the love of nature: we want to get our actions in sync with our ideas. It's time to leave the city and close the curtains of the forest over speechifying.

The cabin, realm of simplification. Beneath the pines, life is reduced to vital gestures, and time spared from daily chores is spent in rest, contemplation, small pleasures. The array of things to be done has shrunk. Reading, drawing water, cutting wood, writing, pouring tea: such things become liturgies. In the city, each action takes place to the detriment of a thousand others. The forest draws together what the city disperses.

FEBRUARY 19

It's evening, it's nine o'clock, I'm at the window. A timid moon is out looking for a kindred spirit, but the sky is empty. I who used to pounce on every second to make it surrender and give up its all—I am learning the art of contemplation. The best way to observe a monastic calm is to find oneself obliged to do so. To sit at the window drinking tea, allowing the land to ripple through its nuances, letting oneself steep in the passing hours, no longer thinking of anything, but suddenly seizing a passing idea and jotting it down in a notebook. The use of a window: to invite beauty in and let inspiration out.

I spend two hours in the position of Dr. Gachet as painted by Van Gogh: gazing into space, cradling his cheek in his hand.

A rumbling arises abruptly in the silence and searchlights punch holes in the night. Through my binoculars I can see a small pack of four-wheel-drive vehicles heading north on the ice—and they're coming my way. Twenty minutes later, eight 4×4s with ad posters on their flanks are lined up on my beach. Some notables have arrived from Irkutsk, members of Putin's party, Yedinaya Rossiya (United Russia), who are spending a week touring the lake. They'll pass the night here in a tent. A few months later, I'll learn that among them are an FSB man, a few guys close to the governor, and the director of a conservation area.[2] Their tires have broken up the snow embankment that led to the shore. The men don't seem to have any respect for the powder snow. Walking on snow, that's attacking the virginity of the world. You start with smashing in the white slopes and before you know it, you're disemboweling Poles.

The engines are running. The transistor radios blare out some Nadiya, a Lolita for preteen global villagers over whom the provincial nouveaux riches in Russia fawn like groupies. I'm devastated.

Shut tight inside my cabin, I try to soothe my nerves with half a pint of Kedrovaya vodka. I can hear those guys whooping out on the ice, where they've cut a hole, set up a spotlight, and are taking turns plunging screaming into the frigid water. Which barely ranks as a first-class hazing in a barracks in Chechnya.

What I came here to escape has descended on my island: noise, ugliness, testosteronic herd behavior. And I, poor fool, with my speeches about retrenchment and my copy of Rousseau's *Reveries* on the table! I think about those Benedictine monks obliged to shepherd tourists around: religious recluses who thought to safeguard their faith in cloisters and who find themselves explaining the rules of their order to indifferent crowds.

In the fourth century, the Desert Fathers became crazed with solitude.[3] Unable to bear even the slightest intrusion, they went deep into the sandy wastes, burying themselves in grottoes. The world they loved was cleansed of their fellow men. These days, sometimes a man just starts shooting at a bunch of kids hanging out in the projects. He gets a short paragraph in the newspapers and lands in a prison cell.

To cool my blood down, I go out on the lake while the Russians are skijoring, being pulled along on skis by their cars. I walk about a mile in the direction of Buryatia and stretch out on the ice. I'm lying on a liquid fossil twenty-five million years old. The stars overhead are a hundred times that. Me, I am thirty-seven, and I'm calling it a day because it's −30° F.

FEBRUARY 20

The men leave, the animals return.

What makes me happier this morning? The departure of that sad bunch of revelers at eight a.m. or the visit of a Siberian titmouse at my window a few minutes later?

I get out of bed so hungover I'm almost upside down. Yesterday I drank to forget. I feed the titmouse, light the stove. The cabin warms up quickly. I install the solar panels on the sawhorses I built yesterday. These panels will have it easy, lying there all day surrounded by beauty, gorging on photons.

Many reflections are born of the steam from my tea.

Sitting with my cup, I wonder about my little sister. Has she had her child yet? I can't receive the slightest news: the computer imploded yesterday, done in by the extreme temperatures, and as for my satellite phone, it doesn't pick up anything. Before I left Paris, I wasted precious hours gathering my technological equipment. I should have heeded the philosophy of Dersu Uzala, the Siberian hunter in Kurosawa's film: the only things you can trust in the forest are an ax, a stove, and a dagger. Without my computer, I have only thought. Well, memory is an electric impulse like any other.

FEBRUARY 21

It's −26° F. Crystalline sky. In cold winters in Norway, water freezes into huge castles around waterfalls, and like the ceiling of the ice palace in the novel by Tarjei Vesaas, the Siberian winter is sterile and pure.

Yesterday's jackasses have trashed everything. They've trampled the drifts and left their mark all over. I won't have peace until a snowstorm reupholsters the lakeshore.

About fifty yards south of my cabin is a *banya*, the Slavic version of a sauna. This one is sixteen by sixteen feet and heated by a stove. Volodya built it last year. It takes four hours to reach 175° F. The banya illustrates the Russian's contempt for temperance. The body swings without transition from fire to ice. After cooking for twenty minutes, I go outside, where it's now −22°, and all that heat evaporates, so with my skull in a vise of ice, I have to go back inside. The *banya*, allegory of our lives spent in the perpetual pursuit of improvement. We push through the door, thinking to reach happiness, but quickly head back where we came from, which will soon oppress us afresh.

In Russia people take refuge in the *banya* once or twice a week to rid themselves of toxins. The heat squeezes the body like a lemon. All rancor dissolves. Bad fat, dirt, and alcohol seep out.

A storm blows in at six in the evening. Naked in my felt boots, I trudge back to the cabin, kerosene lantern in hand. I still remember the story of those *zeks,* those prisoners in the gulag who went out to piss one night in a blizzard. They got lost, couldn't find their way back to the shelter, and were found dead in the morning fifty yards from the barracks. I drink down a quart of piping hot tea. The *banya*: absolute luxury. I'm a new man. Give me a shovel and a red silk scarf and I'd build socialism.

In the evening, a bowl of rice au Tabasco, half a sausage, a pint of vodka, and for dessert the moon up over the mountains, trundling its *tristesse*. I go outside to salute the big maternal ball that watches over the sleep of hermits, then go to bed full of pity for animals that have no cabin or *banya*. Or burrow.

FEBRUARY 22

Life in the forest: escapism? That's how people mired in routine disparage the vital, creative force of life. A game? Absolutely! What else would you call willingly staying alone on a lakeshore by a forest with a crate of books and some snowshoes? A quest? Too big a word. An experiment? In the scientific sense, yes. The cabin is a laboratory, where you precipitate your longings for freedom, silence, and solitude. An experimental field where you invent a slowed-down life for yourself.

The theorists of ecology extol de-growth. Since we cannot continue to aim for endless growth in a world of increasingly scarce resources, we ought to decelerate our rhythms, simplify our existence, reconsider our requirements on the downswing. We can accept these changes of our own accord. Tomorrow, economic crises will force them upon us.

De-growth will never be a political option. Only an enlightened despot could impose such a remedy, and what leader would be brave enough to try? How would he convince his people of the virtue of asceticism? And persuade billions of Chinese, Indians, and Europeans that it's better to read Seneca than to gobble cheeseburgers? The waning utopia: a poetic recourse for those seeking better living through dietetics.

The cabin is a perfect terrain in which to build a life founded on luxurious sobriety. The sobriety of the hermit is not to encumber yourself with either objects or your fellow man. And to break the habits of your former needs.

The luxury of the hermit is beauty. Wherever you look, there is absolute glory. The parade of hours is uninterrupted (aside from yesterday's contretemps). Technology does not imprison you within its circle of fire through the needs it creates.

Retreating to the forest cannot be everyone's course. Hermitism is elitism. Aldo Leopold says as much in his *Sand County Almanac*, which I began rereading this morning right after lighting the stove: "All conservation of wildness is self-defeating, for to cherish we must see and fondle, and when enough have seen and fondled, there is no wilderness left to cherish." When crowds enter the forests, it's to chop them down. Life in the woods is no solution to ecological problems. The phenomenon contains its own counter-principle: the masses, taking to the woods, would bring along the evils they'd hoped to flee by leaving the city. No exit.

A blank day. A fisherman's truck in the distance. Long conversation with my window. In late morning I toss a half-dozen bottles of Kedrovaya into a snowbank. I'll find them again in three months, at the spring thaw. Their necks will peek out of the snow, announcing better weather more surely than snowdrops. Winter's present to the eternal return of spring.

An afternoon of repairs and tidying up. I finish sorting through the crate of provisions and waterproof the cabin's porch roof by nailing up some planks. But afterward? When there are no more planks to nail up or things to put away?

The sun disappears at five behind the mountaintops. Shadows take over the clearing and the cabin grows dark. I find an immediately effective remedy for anguish: a short stroll on the ice. A simple glance at the horizon convinces me of the strength of my choice: this cabin, this life. I don't know if beauty will save the world. It saves my evening.

FEBRUARY 23

Journey into the Whirlwind is the English title of Eugenia Ginzburg's story of her years in the gulag, but in French it's called *Le Vertige*, Vertigo. I read a few pages in the warmth of my sleeping bag. When I awaken, my days line up, eager virgins, offered in blank pages. And I have dozens of them in reserve. Each second of them belongs to me. I'm free to dispose of them as I will, to make them into chapters of light, of slumber, or of melancholy. No one can change the course of such an existence. These days are creatures of clay to be modeled. I am the master of an abstract menagerie.

I was familiar with the vertical vertigo of the climber clinging to the cliff in terror at the sight of the abyss. I remembered the horizontal vertigo of the traveler on the steppe, staggered by vanishing perspectives. I'd experienced the vertigo of the drunkard who thinks he's come up with a brilliant idea that his brain just won't process even though he can sense it growing within him. And I discover the vertigo of the hermit, the fear of the temporal void. The same pang of distress as on the cliff—only not for what lies below, but for what lies ahead.

I am free to do anything in a world where there is nothing to do. I look at the icon of Saint Seraphim. He had God.

God, never sated with the prayers of men, is a helluva pastime. Me? I have writing.

A walk on the lake, after my morning tea. The constant severe cold has the thermometer in its grip, so the ice has stopped cracking. I head out onto the lake. In the snow, with a stick, I trace the first poem in a series of "snow haiku":

> *Footsteps dot the snow*
> *Walking sets short black stitches*
> *Into the white cloth.*

The advantage of poetry inscribed in the snow is that it will not last: verses carried off by the wind.

A mile and a half from the lake's edge, a fault has split the ice. Translucent blocks straddle the fracture, a stripe that darts off parallel to the shoreline. Gurgling wells up from the opening: Baikal is suffering. I walk along the wound, at a distance, for the slightest misstep would slip me underwater.

Suddenly I can picture those dear to me: through the mysterious mechanics of memory, faces spring to mind. Solitude is a country inhabited by the remembrance of others; thinking of them is a comfort in their absence. My dear ones are there, enfolded in memories. I see them. Orthodox Christians believe that Being becomes present in the image. God's essence flows down into the substance of icons, incarnate in glowing oil paint. The picture is transmuted.

Back in the cabin, I decide it's time to set up my altar. With my handsaw I cut a board a foot long and four inches wide, which I nail up next to my work table and christen with three images of Saint Seraphim of Sarov, purchased in Irkutsk. Fifteen years alone in a forest in Western Russia taught Seraphim how to feed bears and speak the language of stags. Next to him I place three icons: Saint Nicholas, a black Virgin, and Tsar Nicholas II, canonized by the Patriarch Alexis and portrayed in his imperial finery. I light a candle and a Partagás no. 4. Through the smoke from my Havana, I watch the candlelight gleam like honey on the picture frames. The cigar: profane incense.

I have finished the chores of settling into my cabin. I've stashed away everything from my last crate. I smoke lying on my back and musing on the fact that I forgot to bring just one thing: a handsome history of painting to help me contemplate, from time to time, a human face.

To remind me of which, I have only my mirror.

FEBRUARY 24

This morning, a clean-slate day. The lake—"the sacred sea," as the Russians call it—is drowning in sky. The thermometer reads −8° F. I light the woodstove and open Casanova's *Story of My Life*. Rome, Naples, Florence parade by, along with Tiretta in his alcove and Henriette in her attic.[4] Then come mad dashes in mail coaches, escape from the ducal prisons of Venice, letters in ink blotched by tears, promises broken as soon as they're given, eternal love sworn twice in the same evening to two different people, and grace, frivolity, style. I learn by heart the phrase in which Giacomo describes a sensual pleasure that "ceased only when it could not possibly increase." I close the book, pull on my felt boots, and go out to draw two buckets of water from my hole in the ice while thinking about Bellino-Teresa of Rome and Leonilda of Salerno.

The books of a dandy and the life of a muzhik.

The day stretches out before me. In Paris I never dwelled much on my state of mind. Life wasn't conducive to tracking the seismographic data of the soul. Here, in the whited-out silence, I have time to perceive the nuances of my own tectonics. The hermit faces this question: can one stand living with oneself?

The captivating spectacle of what's happening outside the window. How can anyone still have a TV at home?

The titmouse is back. I look it up in my bird book. According to the Swedish author, Lars Svensson, born in 1941 and whose oeuvre includes many works like the *famous* guide to the passerines of Europe, the Willow Titmouse may be recognized by its cry of *zee-zee teh teh teh*. Mine's not letting out a peep. One of its relatives, I read on the next page, goes by the name of the Somber Titmouse.

The little creature's visit enchants me. Lights up my afternoon. Within only a few days, I have managed to be content with such a spectacle. Amazing how quickly one can shuck off the Barnum & Bailey business of city life. When I think how I had to fling myself into action with meetings, must-reads, and visits just to get through a Parisian day. And here I am silly-faced over a bird! Maybe life in a log cabin is a regression. But what if I'm making progress through this regression?

FEBRUARY 25

I set out at noon into the wind. I'm going to visit my neighbor, Volodya, a gamekeeper stationed out on Cape Elohin, just over nine miles north of my cabin. He lives in an *izba* with his wife, Irina. Their domain marks the northern frontier of the Baikal-Lena Nature Preserve. I met him five years ago while touring the icy landscapes of the lake on a Ural sidecar motorcycle. I'd loved that flat skull of his, bristling with hair. I'll enjoy seeing him again. I remember his grip: the mitts of a metallurgist, two paddles that crush your hand.

Beyond the cape that protects my cabin, the blustering wind veers northward. The cedars thrash their treetops in the blast, signaling like castaways. Who comes to the rescue of trees?

I hadn't anticipated that the wind would rise. I cut across the lake, toward Elohin, keeping between a half-mile and a mile from the shore. I'm muffled in my Canadian Goose parka (designed for −40° F), a neoprene face mask, a mountaineering mask, and mittens for an arctic expedition. It took me twenty minutes to get suited up. It's vital not to leave even the slightest bit of skin exposed.

Today Baikal has come down with sclerosis. The snow is peeling off, bitten away by the wind, leaving the obsidian ice spotted here and there with patches as white as the skin of an orca, while the lake blackens as it's stripped bare.

My crampons dig into the lacquer. Without them, the gusts would blow me "out to sea." Their powerful sweep courses down mountains, dusting off the taiga. Volodya will tell me later that they can reach seventy-five miles an hour. The wind forces me to walk hunched over. Sometimes a gust simply stops me dead.

I stare out at the section of ice framed in the opening of my hood ruff of coyote fur. Gossamer strands of snow meander across the mirror with the grace of gorgons. Along refrozen faults, the seams are turquoise, the color of lagoons. Then the tropical interlude gives way to a long pool of smoked glass. The sun diffuses streaks of albumin through the fissures. Air bubbles are trapped in the stratum, and one hesitates to step on these pearly jellyfish. Aquatic visions ripple through my face mask, lingering on my retinas when I close my eyes.

At the third hour, I risk looking into the wind, toward the mountains to the west. Trees stand guard until the mountain shrugs them off at about 3,000 feet; canyons wind their way through the drapery of slopes. In four months, they'll channel meltwater down into the bowl. Whenever I come abreast of them, the wind redoubles in strength, from the funnel effect. To think that writers dare depict the beauty of such places....

I've read practically all of Jack London, Grey Owl, Aldo Leopold, Fenimore Cooper, a host of works by American nature writers, and I've never in reading a single one of those pages felt one tenth of the emotion that fills me before these shores. And yet I'll keep on reading, and writing.

Two or three times an hour, a sharp *crack* breaks up my thoughts. The lake is shattering along a fault line. Like surf, birdsong, or the roar of waterfalls, the crumpling of an ice mass won't keep us awake. A motor running, or someone snoring, or water dripping off a roof, on the other hand, is unbearable.

I can't help thinking of the dead. The thousands of Russians swallowed up by the lake.[5] Do the souls of the drowned struggle to the surface? Can they get past the ice? Do they find the hole that opens up to the sky? Now there's a touchy subject to raise with Christian fundamentalists.

It took me five hours to reach Elohin. Volodya welcomed me with a hug and a "Hello, neighbor." Now there are seven or eight of us around the wooden table dunking cookies in our tea: some fishermen passing through, myself, and our hosts. We talk about our lives and I'm exhausted already. Intoxicated by the potluck company, the fishermen argue, constantly correcting one another with grand gestures of disgust and jumping down one another's throats. Cabins are prisons. Friendship doesn't survive anything, not even togetherness.

Outside the window, the wind keeps up its nonsense. Clouds of snow rush by with the regularity of phantom trains. I think about the titmouse. I miss it already. It's crazy how quickly one becomes attached to creatures. I'm seized with pity for these struggling things. The titmice stay in the forest in the icy cold; they're not snobs like swallows, which spend the winter in Egypt.

After twenty minutes, we fall silent, and Volodya looks outside. He spends hours sitting in front of the window pane, his face half in shadow, half bathed in the light off the lake. The light gives him the craggy features of some heroic foot soldier. Time wields over skin the power water has over the earth. It digs deep as it passes.

Evening, supper. A heated conversation with one of the fishermen, in which I learn that Jews run the world (but in France it's the Arabs); Stalin, now there was a real leader; the Russians are invincible (that pipsqueak Hitler bit off more than he could chew); communism is a top-notch system; the Haitian earthquake was triggered by the shockwave from an American bomb; September 11 was a Yankee plot; gulag historians are unpatriotic; and the French are homosexuals.

I think I'm going to space out my visits.

FEBRUARY 26

Volodya and Irina live like tightrope walkers. They have no contact with the inhabitants on the other side of Baikal. No one crosses the lake. The opposite shore is another world, the one where the sun rises. Fishermen and inspectors living north or south of this station sometimes visit my hosts, who rarely venture into the mountains of their domain. They stay along the shoreline, at their outpost in the littoral zone, in equilibrium between the forest and the lake.

This morning Irina proudly shows me her library. In old editions from the Soviet era, she has works by Stendhal, Walter Scott, Balzac, Pushkin. The most recent book is *The Da Vinci Code*. A slight downswing in civilization.

And I go home by walking on the water.

FEBRUARY 27

The luxury of living alone in this world where *being side by side* will become the major problem. In Irkutsk, I learned that a French author had published a long novel entitled *Ensemble, c'est tout*. "Togetherness, It's Everything." It's a lot. It's even the essential challenge, which I don't believe we are meeting very well. The animal and vegetable biological organisms exist together in equilibrium. They destroy one another and reproduce within a greater, well-regulated harmony. Thanks to our frontal cortex, humans cannot manage to coexist in peace. Our music is out of tune.

It's snowing. I'm reading *Men Possessed by God*, Jacques Lacarrière's essay on eremitism in the Egyptian deserts in the fourth century. Dazzled by the sun, hirsute prophets abandoned their families for the desert, where they dragged out their lives in the Thebaid, the territory around ancient Thebes in Egypt. God never visited them there because, like any normal person, he preferred the magnificence of Byzantine domes. The anchorites wished to escape the temptations of their century, but some of them sinned through pride by confusing wariness toward their time with contempt for their fellow men. Not one of the anchorites returned to the world after tasting the poisonous fruit of the solitary life.

Societies do not like hermits and do not forgive them for their flight. They disapprove of the solitary figure throwing his "Go on without me" in everyone else's face. To withdraw is to take leave of one's fellows. The hermit denies the vocation of civilization and becomes a living reproach to it. He is a blot on the social contract. How can one accept this person who crosses the line and latches on to the first passing breeze?

At four in the afternoon, an impromptu visit from Yura. He's the meteorologist at the Uzuri weather station on Olkhon, the largest island in Lake Baikal.

The ice has opened up where it meets the beach: four feet of water are preventing vehicles from crossing to land. New snow has made my shore pristine again. Yura parks his van at the edge of the fracture. He's taking an Australian woman, a tourist, around the lake.

I set the vodka glasses on the table, and we become gently drunk in the fetal warmth. The Australian woman doesn't quite get the picture. We have a brief exchange in English.

"Do you have a car?" she asks.

"No," I reply.

"A TV?"

"No."

"What if you have a problem?"

"I walk."

"Do you go to the village for food?"

"There is no village."

"Do you wait for a car on the road?"

"There is no road."

"Are those your books?"

"Yes."

"Did you write all of them?"

I prefer people whose character resembles a frozen lake to those who are more like marshes. The former are cold and hard on the surface, yet deep, roiling and alive underneath, whereas the latter seem soft, spongy, but inert and impermeable at the core.

The Australian appears leery of sitting on the upended logs I use as stools. She gives me strange looks. My untidiness must reinforce her opinions of the backwardness of the French people. When my guests leave, I'm as tight as a tick and it's time to do some ice skating.

Yesterday's wind has polished the rink. I glide over the glaze with the grace of a seal. Internal faults sheet through the ice in turquoise veils. I pass refrozen fissures the color of ivory. I maintain my balance, skating on the reflections of mountains that resemble shy dancers, cinched into their white dresses and hesitating to join the waltz.

Just before I catch a blade in a crack and crash onto the dance floor, I think about those athletic figure skaters in their tight spangled boleros who zip around whirling pink young Czech partners over their heads for a jury of old ladies who resemble escapees from a Riviera casino, busy brandishing little cards with numbers whose total will win the athlete either a kiss from the girl or chilly tears.

I hobble miserably home with bruised ankles.

In the evening, the sky clears and the temperature plummets. I spend a heavenly hour, swaddled in my bedding, on my wooden bench: a pine plank nailed to two stumps. I'm sitting at the edge of the forest, beneath the tree outside my southern window. Harassed by the western wind, the branches bend down toward the lake, forming a band shell. And in my alcove of icy needles providing an illusion of warmth, I gaze at the black well of the lake. I see the mass of ice as a nightmarish crucible. I sense the force at work beneath this lid. Down in this vault, a universe teems with creatures that slice, crush, and devour. Sponges slowly wave their arms in the depths. Shells coil their spires, beating time to Time and creating nacreous jewels shaped like constellations. At the muddy bottom prowl silurids, monstrous catfish, while carnivorous fish migrate toward the surface in a nightly feast and holocaust of crustaceans. Shoals of Arctic char perform their benthic choreography. Bacteria churn and digest debris, purifying the lake. This bleak working of the waters takes place in silence, beneath a mirror where the stars haven't even the strength to send down their reflections.

FEBRUARY 28

Force 8 this morning. The blasts carry off the snow, slamming it in angry clouds against the greenish-bronze wall where the cedar forest begins. Two hours of housekeeping. Cabin life fosters the same finickiness as does life on a small boat. Mustn't end up like those sailors for whom being shipshape becomes an end in itself and who rot at permanent anchor in port, spending their days tidying an extinguished life.

Setting up residence in a one-room Siberian hut is a victory in the battle against being buried alive by objects. Life in the woods melts the fat away. Unburdened, the airship of life sails higher. Two thousand years ago, the Indo-Sarmatian steppe nomads knew enough to transport their possessions in a small wooden coffer. One's attachment to belongings is

in direct proportion to their rarity, and to a Siberian woodsman, a knife and a gun are as precious as any flesh-and-blood
companion. An object that has been with us through the ups
and downs of life takes on substance and a special aura; the
years give it a protective patina. To learn to love each one of
our poor patrimony of objects, we have to spend a long time
with them. Soon the loving looks directed at the knife, the
teapot, and the lamp come to embrace their materials and
elements: the wood of the spoon, the candle's wax, the flame
itself. As the nature of objects reveals itself, I seem to pierce
the mysteries of their essence. I love you, bottle; I love you,
little jackknife, and you, wooden pencil, and you, my cup,
and you, teapot steaming away like a ship in distress. Outside
roars such fury of wind and cold that if I don't fill this cabin
with love, it might be blown apart.

I learn via my satellite phone, miraculously reactivated,
that my sister's child has been born. This evening I'll drink
to the baby's health and pour a mug of vodka on this Earth
that welcomes one more little creature foisted upon it without permission.

POEM: ON SNOW
For a domain, a bay;
For a castle, a cabin;
For a Fool, a titmouse;
For subjects, my memories.

Spent the morning cutting firewood. It's stacked in a
small but growing wall under the porch roof. I've got ten days'
worth of heating in those split logs.

A hermit expends intense physical energy. In life, we have
the choice of putting machines to work or setting ourselves

to the task. In the first instance, we entrust the satisfaction of our needs to technology. Relieved of all impetus toward effort, we devitalize ourselves. In the second case, we activate the machinery of our bodies to provide for all necessities. And the less we rely on machines, the more muscle we put on. Our bodies toughen up, our skin grows calloused, and our faces weather. Energy redistributes itself, transferring from the belly of machines to the human body. Backwoodsmen are power stations glowing with dynamic force. When they enter a room, their vitality fills the space.

After a few days, I noticed the first changes in my body. My limbs are more muscular, but I've got the flabby abdomen and white skin of an alcoholic or a creature dwelling in a mud bank. Less tension, slower heartbeat: confined in a cramped space, I'm learning to move slowly. Even the mind grows lax. Without conversation, deprived of the contradiction and sarcasm of sparring partners, the hermit is less witty, less lively and incisive, less worldly, slower off the mark than a city dweller. The hermit gains in poetry what is lost in agility.

Sometimes, this desire to do nothing. I've been sitting at my table for an hour, surveying the progress of sunbeams across the tablecloth. Light ennobles all it touches even glancingly: wood, the row of books, the knife handles, the curve of a face and of time going by, even the dust motes in the air. That's not nothing, to be specks of dust in this world.

So now I'm rhapsodizing about dust. March is going to be a long month.

❦❦❦❦❦❦❦❦❦❦❦❦❦❦❦❦❦❦❦❦❦❦❦❦❦❦❦❦❦❦❦❦❦❦❦❦

Time

MARCH 1

My father's birthday. I imagine the festive dinner back home near Guise, in Picardy. Every year the family gathers in a restaurant remodeled from eighteenth-century stables: the Belgian cousins, beer, wine, meat, and the light beaming down from the brick vaults. They must have arrived in the rain and are now dining cozily. The tables are set up beneath the racks where the animals once tucked into their feed. Hundreds of horses that would be warm in these stalls now spend the night outside in northern France. I'm no fonder of stables turned into banquet halls than I am of churches turned into munitions dumps. I pour myself a generous shot of vodka, raise a toast toward the west, and toss it down.

Would my father be happy here? He wouldn't like all this nature. He loves the theater, public debate, lively conversation. He is at home in the world of the snappy rejoinder. It's hard to hold a conversation in the woods of Siberia. There's nothing to stop a man from expressing himself, of course. He can always roar like the fellow in *The Howling Miller*, a tale by the Finnish novelist Arto Paasilinna. It's just that yelling is futile. From a naturalist perspective, the rebellious figure of *l'homme révolté* is useless. The sole virtue, in these latitudes, is acceptance. Vide the Stoics, animals, or (even better!) simple stones. The taiga can offer only two things: its resources, which we blithely plunder, and its indifference. Let's take the moon, for example. Yesterday it was shining. In my notebook I wrote, *The rhinoceros moon that with its horn wounds a night the color of Africa.* Just how much of a damn does the moon give about such sophomoric pseudo-aphorisms?

Tonight I finished a murder mystery. I closed the book feeling as if I'd just eaten at McDonald's: nauseated and slightly ashamed. The action is hectic—and forgotten the next moment. Four hundred pages to find out whether MacDouglas cut up MacFarlane with a butter knife or an ice ax. The characters are ruled by all-powerful facts. The myriad details paper over a void. Is it because novels like these resemble bureaucratic blather that they're called police procedurals?

Midnight; I stroll out on the lake. How can I recover the impression I had when I first arrived on these gleaming coal-gray shores seven years ago? My soul was laid wide open with happiness. Where is the *enjoyment of this place* that kept me awake those first few nights on the beach? The comfort of my cabin is dulling my perceptions. Too much ease coats the soul with soot. I've been here just a few weeks, and already I feel like a local. Soon I'll know every evergreen as well as I know the bistros of my Parisian stomping grounds. Being at home somewhere is the beginning of the end.

A hundred paces from my cabin, the toilet: a hole in the ground in an open shed cobbled together from planks. Going out there tonight, I remember "The Apple Tree," a short story by Daphne du Maurier: a man meets his downfall one freezing night, tripping over the roots of his long-suffering wife's favorite tree, vengefully cut down by the widower after her death. I imagine myself falling somewhere along the way in minus thirty degrees. I would die there, about fifty yards from the cabin, with its string of smoke rising from the roof, and the explosions of the lake ice for a eulogy. Ceasing to struggle, I would slowly rejoin the beautiful silence while thinking: No, really, *this is too dumb.* Oh, those people who've gotten lost and died a few yards from shelter. . . .

Help is there, a mere ten steps away, but the threshold of safety remains out of reach. Kurosawa made a movie about that: a group of mountaineers, freezing in a blizzard some seventy yards from camp. And Scott of the Antarctic! Have we forgotten his agony, not even twelve miles from a supply depot? Out in the Taklamakan Desert of northwest China, where ancient mummies of Caucasoid peoples have been discovered in the Tarim Basin, the explorer Sven Hedin had the opposite adventure: believing himself lost, he prepared to die—and stumbled onto an oasis.

MARCH 2

Almost half a mile to the south of the cabin, a granite rise cleaves the forest. Looming three hundred feet into the air, the rise dominates the lake; six larches crown the summit, giving it the shape of a pine cone. Lynx tracks mottle the slope leading to the foot of the dome. I toil my way up there; powdery snow covers the scree. I sink in up to my thighs and sometimes lose a foot down a gap between two rocks. From the summit, Baikal: a plain striped with ivory veins. The silence of the forest envelops the world, and the echo of this silence is millions of years old. I'll be coming back here. The "pinecone" will be my crow's nest for the days when I need a lofty view.

Sasha and Yura, the fishermen I met at Sergei's two weeks ago, drop in for a visit. I pour the ritual glasses. In this life, sharing a glass with a companion, feeling safe in the warmth of a shelter—this is already something. The stove is drawing well and the atmosphere makes us drowsy. A soft weight falls upon our brows, a sign of biological well-being. The vodka goes down. The spirit is buoyed, the body contented. The air fills with tobacco smoke as conversation dies away. I always find peace in the company of Russian woodsmen: I feel theirs is the human environment in which I would have liked to be born. It's good not to have to keep a conversation going. Why is life with others so hard? Because you must always find something to say. I think of those days of walking around Paris nervously tossing off "Just-fine-thank-yous" and "Let's-get-together-soons" to strange people I don't know who babble the same things to me, as if in a panic.

"Cold?" asks Sasha after a moment.

"S'okay," I say.

"Snow?"

"Plenty!"

"Visitors?"

"Day before yesterday."

"Sergei?"

"No, Yura Uzov."

"Ah, that Yura . . ."

"Yes, that's the one."

There are dialogues like this in Jean Giono's *Song of the World*. At the beginning of the novel, the riverman, Antonio, addresses the forester, Matelot:

"That's life," said Antonio.

"S'better, the forest," said Matelot.

"Each to his own," said Antonio.

"The less you talk, the longer you live," says Yura. I don't know why, but I suddenly think of a certain garrulous French politician. Must tell him he's in danger.

Sasha leaves me a five-liter keg of beer. In the evening I slowly dispatch two of those liters. Beer or the local dive, the alcohol of the poor. Beer is a sedative that anesthetizes thought and dissolves all spirit of revolt. With the beer hose, totalitarian states extinguish all of society's fires. Nietzsche loathed this piss-juice because it fostered "the spirit of heaviness."

With a stick in the snow:

The world, for which we are in turn the brush or the brushstroke.

MARCH 3

I remember my walking trips in the Himalayas, traveling on horseback in the Celestial Mountains, biking three years ago on the Ustyurt Plateau of Central Asia.... That joy, then, at conquering a mountain pass. The carnivorous hunger for covering the miles. The longing to press on even if it kills you. At times I advanced as if possessed, walking into exhaustion, delirium. In the Gobi, I would stop to spend the night *right there*, crumpling where I stood, and set out again the next day automatically, the moment I opened my eyes. I was aping a wolf; now I'm being a bear. I want to dig in, become the earth after having been the wind. I was obsessively bound to movement, drugged with space. I was chasing after time, believing it was hiding just over the horizon. "The vigorous use of time may offset its fast pace" (Montaigne, *Essays*, vol. 3.), and that's how I dealt with its swift passage.

A free man possesses time. A man who dominates space is merely powerful. In cities, the minutes, hours, and years are the flowing blood of wounded time, and they escape us. In the cabin, time grows calm. It lies at your feet like a good old dog, and suddenly you've even forgotten it's there. I am free because my days are.

As I do each morning while the stove is heating up, I go down to the water hole thirty yards out from the shore. The opening freezes over during the night and must be chopped free again. I stand there a moment, gazing at the taiga. Out of the hole flashes a white hand that grabs my ankle in a blinding hallucination—these waters have swallowed so many drowned bodies!—and I recoil, dropping the ice ax. My heart is racing. Sleeping waters are wicked: lakes exhale a melancholy atmosphere because spirits prowl there bottled up, brooding on their grief. Lakes are burial vaults, where silt gives off a noxious odor and vegetation clumps in dark reflections. Out at sea, the currents, salt, and ultraviolet light dissolve all mystery in limpid waters.

What happened in this bay? Was there a shipwreck, or some settling of scores? I have no intention of cohabiting for six months with a soul in torment. I've got my hands full with my own. Lugging my two buckets, I return to the warmth of the cabin; through the window, the water hole makes a black stain on the pale ice sheet, a dangerous spy-hole between two worlds.

Every afternoon I put on my snowshoes. After a ninety-minute tramp into the trees, I reach the upper skirt of the forest.

I like entering the woods. Sounds soon fade away. When I step inside a Gothic cathedral in France or Belgium, I feel the same soothing calm, a sweetness of being that diffuses its warmth behind the brow and makes eyelids heavy. Something in me reacts to the glow of both limestone and conifers. At present, I prefer old-growth forests to the stone naves of churches.

Beneath the trees, forever sheltered from the wind, the snow lies thick. I sink deeply into it in spite of my snowshoes. Lynxes, wolves, minks, and foxes roam at night. The tracks tell stories of tragedy in the wild. Some are beaded with blood; they are the words of the forest. The animals tread lightly on their paws in proportion to their weight, whereas man is too heavy to walk atop snow. Now and then, the cries of jays; otherwise, silence. They call from the crowns of firs, feathered sentinels on needle-thin towers. They call because I have invaded their home. No one ever asks animals' permission to cross their domain.

Lichen hangs from the trees. Long ago I read a tale in which the author imagined a god who roamed the understory of the forest, where his coat would catch on branches, leaving shreds that became lichen.

The sadness of the pines: they look cold. After an hour of climbing, I check my altimeter: 2,461 feet. Another effort, and beyond about 2,950 feet, the forest will lay down its weapons. Up there, snow polished by tempests presents a hard surface. The snowshoes grip well; I progress quickly and choose to go up one of the narrow valleys. A few larches survive beyond the timber line. They are solitary here, with contorted branches that stand out against the blue background of Baikal, starred with fractures. The gold branches, the lapis lazuli of the lake, the white, crazed ice: the palette of Hokusai.

Sometimes the ground gives way. The snow, mounded over a thicket of dwarf pines, collapses beneath my weight, dumping me into a net of branches, where my snowshoes get caught in the tangles. I curse fiercely down in my hole. In *Kolyma Tales*, Varlam Shalamov, a former prisoner in a gulag in Siberia, remembers the dwarf pines that surrounded the camp. When the temperature moderated in May, the trees would free themselves from their blanket of snow: standing up straight again, they were harbingers of spring, and hope.

At an altitude of 3,280 feet, I climb toward the rocky crests that flank the thalweg, that line connecting the lowest points along the length of a valley. Looking down, I see ridges serrated like dorsal fins against the lake. Some of my friends live for this alone: gaining altitudes where the odorless air stings the nose, where life hangs between earth and sky in a realm of abstract forms. When they descend into the valleys once again, they find that life smells bad. Mountaineers are unhappy in cities.

Among the boulders that protrude above the snow, I build a fire to make tea. Side by side, we smoke, the fire and I, offering our spiraling fragrant curls to the ancient lake. During such days up here, I dedicate myself to the pure joy of being: taking a drag, alone, high above the lake; hurting nothing, taking orders from no one, desiring no more than what I experience and knowing that nature does not reject us. In life, three ingredients are necessary: sunshine, a commanding view, and legs aching with remembered effort. Plus some little Montecristos. Happiness is as fleeting as a puff of cigar smoke.

It's −22° F. Too chilly for more contemplation. I select a couloir in which to slide down again, braking by grabbing at ash saplings and dogwood branches. Back in the forest of pines and birches, I plunge into the slumbering snow, take a guess as to the appropriate heading, and regain the lakeshore in an hour, winding up not far from the cabin. When I see it again, I feel welcome and go happily home. I close the door and light the stove. In May, I simply must climb all the way to the summits of my domain.

Hölderlin's epigraph for *Hyperion; or, The Hermit in Greece,* is taken from the epitaph on the tombstone of St. Ignatius of Loyola: "Not to be confined by the greatest, yet to be contained within the smallest, is divine." In short, after an outing, after gorging on the grandeur of the lake, remember to give a little wink to a small servant of beauty: a snowflake, some lichen, a titmouse.

MARCH 4

The sun's caress on the windowpane approaches the sensual delight in the touch of a loved one's hand. When you're off hermiting in the woods, only the sun is allowed to intrude.

To get the day off to a good start, it's important to remember one's duties. In order: greetings to the sun, the lake, and the little cedar growing in front of the cabin, on which, every evening, the moon hangs up its lantern.

I live here in the realm of predictability. Each day goes by, a mirror of the one before, a rough draft of the one to come. The passing hours bring variations in the sky's coloration, the comings and goings of the birds, and a thousand almost imperceptible things. When the world of men goes silent, a fresh tint in the feathery foliage of the cedars or a glinting reflection off the snow becomes a considerable event. I will no longer look down on folks who discuss the rain and sunny skies. Talk about the weather has a cosmic dimension. The subject is no less profound than a debate about Salafist militants infiltrating Pakistani intelligence agencies.

What are unexpected in the lives of hermits are their thoughts, which alone interrupt the course of monotonous hours. To surprise yourself, you must dream.

I remember when I embarked, two years ago, on board the *Jeanne d'Arc*, a training vessel of the French navy. We were returning from Suez, moving slowly through the Mediterranean. Islands and capes drifted by, watched in silence by officers up on the bridge, all rejoicing inside to see each fresh nuance appear in the coastline. Today I look out my window with the same watchfulness as I did aboard the *Jeanne*, attentive now to the shifting shadows and trembling light instead of to changes ashore. Up on the bridge, we asked movement in space to provide us with distraction, while in the cabin, time's tiny precipitations are enough. Immobile, becalmed, I sail on. If anyone asks me what I did during my months here, I will reply, "I went on a cruise."

Inside and outside the cabin, the feeling of time's passage is not the same. Indoors: a rippling of cozy hours. Outdoors: –22° F, the slap of every second. On the ice, the hours drag. The cold numbs their flow. So the threshold of my door is not a wooden slat separating heat from cold and comfort from hostility, but a throttle valve connecting the two halves of an hourglass in which time does not pass at the same speed.

A Siberian cabin is not built to the specifications of the civilized world. Here there are no requirements for security, government assistance, insurance. Russians make a point of never taking precautions. Within a space of ninety-seven square feet, the body moves among the searingly hot stove, the saw hanging from a rafter, the knives and axes planted in the beams. In the Europe of Safety First, these cabins would be razed.

I spend the afternoon sawing up a cedar trunk. Chain-gang work: the wood is dense, the metal teeth don't bite well. A glance toward the south, to catch my breath. The landscape is at rest, perfect, structured: the grand curve of the bays, the sulfurous streaks in the sky, the stilettos of the pines, the majesty of the granitic drapery. The cabin is at the heart of a tanka poem, in contact with the lacustrine, mountainous, and woodland worlds, symbolizing respectively death, the eternal return, and divine purity.

The cedar is slender but must be two hundred years old: here, what living things lose in abundance they gain in intensity; the trees don't explode in luxuriant foliage, but their flesh is as hard as marble.

Another pause. Last year, on the flanks of the Samarga Valley in the Russian Far East, I visited some lumberjack camps. Moscow is selling its taiga to the Chinese. Chainsaws lacerate the silence around the camps, dismembering the forest acre after acre. The invaders slice up the trunks as meticulously as wood-eating insects. Some of these trees are destined for a strange fate: sprung from the soil of a wilderness valley ridge, having weathered a hundred, maybe a hundred and fifty Siberian winters, these cedars will find themselves chopped into chopsticks condemned to stuff soup noodles down the gullets of Shanghai laborers building a shopping mall for expats. Times are hard for fir trees. Sergei told me that up behind the rocky ridges flanking Baikal, deep in the Baikal-Lena Nature Preserve, lumberjacks are already at work.

Russians, so proud of the integrity of their national territory, pay no attention to this underhanded plot. Puffed up with the illusion of living in a limitless country, they imagine their Nature to be inexhaustible. One becomes an ecologist faster in the patchwork mountain pastures of the Swiss Alps than dying of angst in the vastness of the Russian plains.

I also cut down a dead birch; its bark will be useful tinder to get the stove going. The tree's skin is striped with nicks: has a forest spirit been marking off the passing days?

By the time I turn homeward, large snowflakes blanket the bristling ranks of stumps and roots parading along the profile of the scree.

MARCH 5

Another incursion into the upper realm. I'm looking for the waterfall Sergei told me about: "An hour and a half on foot, elevation around 3,300 feet." I'm wandering in my snowshoes along the edge of the scree slope, above the cedar line. At the top of one of the canyons in the mountainside—elevation 3,000—I chance upon the waterfall. The thin ribbon of ice falls from a notch in the summit of a schistose wall, hurling itself into the void and covering the black rock with mother-of-pearl.

Not a single bird calls. Winter has petrified life. The world waits to awaken. The snow, waterfall, clouds, even the silence: all held in suspense. One day, things will get going again. Warmth will come down from the sky, and nature's tissues will swell with the springtime flood. New blood will beat in the animals' veins, the thalwegs will fill with water, sap will flow in the trees. Leaves will pierce the scales of their buds;

the snows will murmur their desire to rush down to the lake; larvae will hatch and insects will emerge from the soil. A tremendous rushing sound will course down the mountainsides. Life will move along the slopes. Animals will head for the lake to drink as summer clouds make their way north. For the moment, though, I am the only creature floundering through the deep powder to get home.

In the evening, ice skating. An hour gliding along the lacquer. Visions slip past: plaques of obsidian, stripes as blue as a lagoon, like a perfume ad from the '80s.

Out on the ice, a tiny island of snow spared by the wind. I collapse there for a cigarillo. The cracking of Lake Baikal sends shudders through my bones. It's good to live near a lake. A lake offers the spectacle of its symmetry (the shores and their reflections) and a lesson in equilibrium (the equation between its affluents and effluents). Miraculous precision is necessary to maintain its hydrographic levels, as each drop entering the basin must be redistributed.

Living in a cabin means having the time to take an interest in such things, the time to write them down, the time to read them over. And what's more, once all that is done, you still have time left over.

At the window this evening, *la mésange, mon ange*: my angel the titmouse.

MARCH 6

I stay in bed this morning. Peeping out from under the comforter, I can see through the window the fat peach hoisting itself over the mountains of Buryatia. One day, the sun will reveal to us where it finds the strength to get up at dawn.

*

A gust of wind shoves an icy draft under the door. A hermit, isolated? But from what? Air slips through the beams, sunshine floods the table, water flows within a stone's throw, humus lies beneath the wooden floor, snow filters in via the pores of the cabin, the scent of the forest percolates through gaps, an insect invites itself in to check out the parquet. In the city a layer of asphalt protects the foot from all contact with the earth, and people are hemmed in by walls of stone.

The lake is booming horrendously. Sitting with my tea, I open my volume of Schopenhauer's *The World as Will and Representation* in the Presses Universitaires de France edition with its orange cover. Back home in Paris, it sat in splendor on my table, where I never dared open it. There are books one circles warily. Basically, I've retired to the woods to finally do what has always intimidated me. In chapter 39, "The Metaphysics of Music," I read these lines: "The deepest notes correspond to the inferior degrees, the inorganic bodies that yet already possess certain properties; the upper register represents for us the plants and animals. . . . All bodies and all organisms must be considered as emerging from the various degrees of evolution of the planetary mass that is both their support and their origin; this is exactly the same relationship that exists between the root of a chord and the upper register." When the lake plays its composition of diffused crackings and detonations, this is what it is: the music of the inorganic and undifferentiated, a melody from the lower depths, the symphony of the world making its long-ago debut. A nameless *something* bubbles and gurgles, while over the *basso continuo* of its convulsions, a snowflake or a titmouse tries out a little tune.

The temperature drops precipitously. I chop down some wood in -31° F, and when I get home, the heat seems like a supreme luxury. After the frigid air, the sound of a vodka cork popping near a cast-iron stove produces infinitely more pleasure than a palatial stay on the Grand Canal in Venice. That huts might rank with palaces is something the habitués of royal suites will never understand. They did not experience the aching of numbed fingers before they learned about bubble baths. Luxury is not a state but the crossing of a line, a threshold beyond which, suddenly, all suffering ceases.

It's noon, quite windy, and I'm off. I'm setting out on foot for the island of Ushkani, eighty-one miles away. I'm allowing three days to reach Sergei's ranger station, then a day to get to the island, a second to stay overnight, a third to get off the island—and three more days to get home. I'm pulling a child's sled loaded with a bag of clothing, some provisions, my skates, Rousseau's *Reveries,* and Jünger's journal, which I began reading yesterday. A humanist philosopher and a Swabian entomologist: serious company.

I traverse chaotic jumbles of ice. Snow has spread white cream over the blue slices; I'm walking on a cake for a boreal god. At times the sun illuminates the tips of icicles, lighting up stars in broad daylight. On the dark, glassy sections, the fault lines run through the obsidian masses in a recurrent pattern, a kind of arboreal schema in right angles, branching out in the manner of genealogical trees or the roots of certain plants. Might that correspond to a mathematical structure, a writing determined by the laws of the Universe? Water has a memory; perhaps ice possesses a form of intelligence (a cold one, of course)?

After six hours of walking, I round a cape and see the hamlet of Zavorotni: a few wooden houses nestled in a bay. Only one is occupied year-round, by a ranger named Volodya E. This place is an enclave about six miles by twelve within the preserve, a free zone where Russians can indulge in their favorite activity: doing whatever they want. The village served as a rear base for the teams of men who worked a microquartz mine in the local mountain at an elevation of 3,300 feet. Microquartz was used in the manufacture of diamond styluses for stereos and the needles in some oscillators. I owe my knowledge of these fascinating things to V.E., who welcomes me into his *izba*.

His kitchen is basically a pigsty. Grease coats the walls. The floor is dangerous: a person might slip on some fish guts and tip over one of the pots full of simmering seal grease intended for the dogs who run riot here. V.E. was for a long time the head of the weather station at Solnechnaya, twenty-five miles to the south. He's a former alcoholic who stopped drinking after a heart attack; he is doing better these days, but his teeth are gone.

He shows me a chunk of lava, a present from some geologists.

"These are the oldest minerals in the world," he tells me.

"How old?"

"Four billion years. I put it under my pillow to inspire my dreams."

"And?"

"Nothing yet."

He adds: "You hungry?"

"Yes."

"You want some fish?"

"Sounds good."

The sight of V.E. busy whacking a frozen fish with a hammer while standing at a kitchen table that hasn't been cleaned since the end of the Soviet Union delights me. Russians never put on airs, and the fish is delicious.

"Anything happen in the world over the last three weeks?" I wonder.

"No, it's quiet, the Muslims are hibernating."

MARCH 7

A day on the lake, fascinated by the designs in the icy mantle. Into that frozen body the cracks and fissures weave electric layers whose current spreads with hectic abandon: the lines retract, join up, veer away. The ice has absorbed the energy of the shocks by distributing it along sheaves of "wiring." Staggering blows rend the silence and are borne along as the echo of an explosion dozens of miles away. The noise vents itself though these networks of veining. As the sun's rays are refracted in the cross-connections, the skein begins to glow. Light irradiates the veins of turquoise, infusing them with trails of gold. The ice convulses. It is alive and I love it. The pearly coils trace knots resembling neuronal tissues or photos of stardust clouds. The map of this meshing would be psychedelic. Without drugs or wine, my brain perceives hallucinatory sequences as the world offers glimpses of an unknown writing. The patterns stream by as if born in an opium dream, for Nature refuses us even the consolation of projecting our own brand-new images on this psychedelic screen.

This oeuvre will vanish in May, engulfed by the thaw. The ice of Baikal is a mandala that will lose its patient design to warmth and the wind.

Twelve and a half miles south of Zavorotni, I spend the night in the cabin of Bolshoi Solontsovi. It's a dilapidated shelter used when needed by the foresters of the preserve. Three years ago, I spent two days here with Maxim, an ex-convict to whom the authorities had given a second chance. They'd made him an inspector. He had the face of a brute and a gentle, sweet smile. He was moping terribly in his cabin, and his life was no cakewalk. A bear had been prowling the clearing for days, trapping him inside the cabin. "I've been reduced to peeing in my teapot," he'd complained. His superiors hadn't wanted to risk issuing a rifle to a former drug addict fresh from the jails of Irkutsk. In the evening, the bear had come and stared at us from the door. "Fucking hell, I was safer in prison," Maxim had fumed.

Since then, the bear has been murdered, Maxim has relapsed, he's serving out a new sentence, and the cabin of Bolshoi Solontsovi is empty once more.

I play chess with myself. The last streak of daylight shoots through the window, ricocheting off a knife blade. In spite of a mad, heroic charge, White loses. On the wooden beams, photos: nude girls with smooth white skin and hefty breasts pose in positions a bit too overdone to inspire any conversation. Already it's impossible to see a thing; nightfall has won out.

MARCH 8

On the ice. I reach the weather station at Solnechnaya during the afternoon. Back in the time of the defunct USSR, a trim little village stood on a deforested shoulder of the mountain. Today the remains of the hamlet harbor two people: Anatoli, an inspector, and Lena, his ex-wife. They recently separated and live in two neighboring *izbas*, like a set of porcelain dogs at the end of the world. A chaotic mess of jagged ice makes it hard to reach the station, and when I knock on Anatoli's door, there is no answer. I push the door open. Sunlight floods into the room. There are empty tin cans on the floor, empty bottles beneath the table, and a body on the couch. I had forgotten it was March 8, Women's Day in Russia. Anatoli has been celebrating. Lena will later tell me that he banged on her door all night shouting, "You're gonna open up!" A gentleman should always observe Women's Day.

I wake him up. He smells of formaldehyde, ether, and cabbage. He stands up and falls down.

"It's my rheumatism," he says, to save face. "Very painful."

"Yes, the damp weather," I agree.

Anatoli spends the afternoon drifting along the steep flank of the mountain. These weather stations are launching pads to psychiatric wards. Ever since Stalin's time, they stud the territory from Belarus to Kamchatka. Spreading such posts around was a way to both occupy the emptiness and maintain a supply of citizens who would warn Moscow if a fascist turned up . . . or if anyone else felt an itch to protest something. In *izbas* all outfitted with the same recording equipment, meteorologists live in couples or groups of four or five. Every three hours, they go outside to record the data they will radio to their base. Their time is not their own, and the inflexible routine fosters mental confusion. This no-exit situation becomes a circus of disorders: the sufferers drink, tear into one another, develop mental pathologies. Once in a while, a disappearance interrupts their routine. On an island station in the Laptev Sea, north of Siberia, a meteorologist's felt boots were found. Conclusion: wool gives polar bears indigestion. A few decades ago, here in Solnechnaya, a stationmaster hated by his men vanished into thin air one winter's night out in the forest. The administration hushed the matter up.

I leave Anatoli when Lena invites me to tea at her place. She has the handsome face of a Flemish fishwife, with blue, almond-shaped eyes and a pert nose. We have three hours before I must set out again. The tea steams and Lena holds forth. She arrived at the station when she was sixteen and wouldn't leave here for anything.

"I don't like asphalt. In the city the tar makes my feet hurt and money evaporates."

"And the job?"

"I like it. Except for the wild animals. The recording equipment is fifty yards from the house and at night, that's a really long way, so I run. But I'm not complaining."

"Why not?"

"Because there are stations where the equipment is more than half a mile away!"

"No animal attacks?"

"Yes, wolves."

"When?"

"The second time I saw the wolf, here, was June 6. I go out to the field at eight o'clock and see the cows running home past me. I thought the ox had frightened them. While I'm coming back, off in the distance I think I see our dog Zarek. I turn around—Zarek is right there. So it's a real wolf, up ahead of me! The cows had already gone around behind me again, so I run at the wolf with a big stone. The wolf comes closer, I see its grin. I'm throwing stones at it. So the cows, maybe they felt ashamed, they do another U-turn and come back to me!"

"The cows came back!"

"And the ox as well. So then the wolf begins to retreat, still grinning, as if it were urging me to follow it. And I do, throwing more stones: I pluck up my courage, and I have a whole herd behind me!"

"Good for the cows."

"Yes, but another year, we had losses."

"More wolves?"

"No, the bears."

"Bears?"

"I hear the dogs howling. Like you wouldn't believe. I run outside to see. Afterward, some women said I was crazy to have gone out alone. If the bear had still been there, it would have killed me. So I go out, I see the ox lying on the ground, dying. His legs were broken, gashes on the muzzle, and a big chunk of flesh torn from around the spine. The bear had broken his legs so he couldn't run away."

"The poor ox!"

"I turned straight around and ran home. I called Palitch, a friend who happened to be around. We had to do something. Palitch finished off the ox with a knife. Me, I didn't eat any of that meat. The next day, we found the cow. . . ."

"The cow?"

"The bear had already stashed her before I arrived. A few hundred yards from where it attacked the ox. It had made a tomb for her. . . . Her belly was slashed open. She'd been pregnant. You could see the calf spilling out, and the cow's muzzle was torn off. Cows, well, I get attached, as if they were children. I had a nervous breakdown that year."

Lena stands up to send a message on the radio, saying, "If I miss three check-in times in a row, it means I'm dead."

I leave her, fortified in my love for Russia, a nation that sends rockets into space and where people fight off wolves with stones.

After walking a good mile over sheets of lunar ice that resemble huge jellyfish veined with turquoise, I reach the station at Pokoyniki, where Sergei and Natasha live. Sergei has prepared a *banya*. We suffocate there for an hour. Then we empty a bottle of honey-flavored vodka, not forgetting to toast the ladies, because March 8, that's the day men buy themselves a good conscience on the cheap.

MARCH 9

At noon, Sergei opens a three-liter bottle of beer. On the label, it says *Siberian Size*.

For five years, I dreamed about this life. Today, it feels like an ordinary accomplishment. Our dreams come true but only as soap bubbles fated to burst.

MARCH 10

I set off for Ushkani. The island lies nineteen miles east of Pokoyniki, out in the middle of the lake. From a distance, it looks like a felt hat sitting on the horizon. The wind is from the northwest. I push on like a maniac, eating up the miles on this lake of frosted glass. A fish swims beneath the ice. We are a world apart. To me, the fish seems imprisoned, cut off from the sky by an impenetrable lid, it's heartbreaking. Sometimes I lie down on a snowbank to look at the hygienically blue sky through the oval frame of my furry hood. My little sled holds me back, but when boosted by a gust of wind, it shoots past me and I have to lean back to stop it. I reach the island in six hours.

The lord and master around here is Yura. He lives with his wife in a weather station on a steep flank of the island: four large *izbas*, facing west. He has the despotic character of island hermits, the "King of Clipperton" syndrome, which becomes tinged with madness when vodka lights its fire in his eyes.[6] He reigns unchallenged in his satrapy. In the outposts of Baikal, the authority of Moscow holds hardly any sway. A tacit contract does link the government to its reclusive citizens: the former sends not a single ruble in subsidy payment, while the latter cheat, lie, and scrounge all they can.

MARCH 11

I spend a whole day on Ushkani Island, half asleep. The Siberian sun warms the facade of the *izba* and light pours into my room. Lying on my bed, I read a French translation of Jünger's *Journal*, vol. 1, 1965–1970. The old magus would not have liked the brightness here; too raw, it kills the mystery of things. The faded eyes of seers are more at home in halftones. I gather images from every page, flashes, visions. Jünger expresses through symbols the metaphysics of the physical world.

P. 27: "Common progress consists of the quantification of things and human beings, translated into numbers."

P. 66: "Human beings must be viewed as semaphores, bearers of signs."

P. 119: "Here dwell gods whose names I need not know, and who lose themselves, like trees in the forest, in the Divine-in-itself."

P. 164: "A single day in Ceylon . . . Perhaps it would be better, instead of allowing ourselves to be dragged from temple to temple, to pay our respects to a few ancient trees."

P. 199: "Demythologizing aims to render people and their conduct submissive to the laws of the world of machines."

P. 266: "The less we cling to differences, the more intuition comes to our aid; we no longer hear the rustling of the tree but the whole forest's answer to the wind."

P. 353: "Entrance fee. Even better, quite often, is the exit fee, the price we pay to have nothing whatsoever to do anymore with society."

P. 366: "Increasing haste is a symptom of the transmutation of the world into numbers."

P. 519: "And one day, bees discovered flowers and molded them to their caresses. Ever since, beauty has filled more space in the world."

Where does it come from, my love for aphorisms, witticisms, and a nicely turned phrase? And my preference for the particular over the collective, individuals over groups? From my name? *Tesson*: "shard," a fragment of something that once was. Its shape conserves the memory of the bottle. A "Tesson" would be a creature nostalgic for a lost unity, seeking to rejoin the All. Which is what I'm doing here, getting drunk in the woods.

Yura is tending to his chores. He will never return to the city. On the island, he enjoys the two ingredients necessary for an unencumbered life: space and solitude. In the city, the human crowd can survive only if its excesses are curbed and its needs regulated by law. When men crowd together, administration is born. An equation as old as the first neolithic hamlet and illustrated in every human collectivity. For the hermit, administrative rule begins with another person. Then it's called marriage.

Men of the forest are very skeptical about projects for "citizen cities," self-governed, no prisons or police, where triumphant liberty shall suddenly reign among crowds now perfectly well behaved. These loners detect a grotesque paradox in such utopias: the city is an inscription in space of culture, order—and their natural child, coercion.

Only withdrawal to a boundless and barely populated wilderness validates a pacifist anarchy founded on this simple principle: in contrast to urban life, danger in the woods arises from Nature, not Man. The idea of majority rule that governs human relations may therefore fail to reach such distant regions. Let's daydream a little. We might imagine for our Western societies small groups of folks, like those in Pokoyniki or Zavorotni, who are eager to peel off from the parade of progress. Tired of overpopulated cities where governance implies the promulgation of ever more abundant rules, hating the administrative hydra, outraged by the intrusion of new technologies into every aspect of daily life, anticipating the spread of social and ethnic chaos fostered by the growth of megaregions, these groups decide to abandon urban zones and return to the woods. They would re-create villages in forest glades among towering trees. They would invent a new life. This impetus would be related to the hippie movement but draw strength from different motives. The hippies fled an order that oppressed them. The neoforesters will flee a disorder that demoralizes them. As for the woods, they are ready to welcome pilgrims, being used to the eternal return.

To attain a sense of inner freedom, one must have solitude and space galore. Add to these the mastery of time, complete silence, a harsh life, and surroundings of geographic grandeur. Then do the math and find a hut.

MARCH 12

I leave the island behind. I sleepwalk the nineteen miles back to Pokoyniki in seven hours. I spend the afternoon on a bench near Sergei's cabin, motionless and muffled up like a little old man. A little old man who just tossed off nineteen miles in -24°F weather.

Sergei joins me, and we talk about the people—English, Swiss, German—who visit the lake in the summer.

"I love the Germans," says Sergei.

"Ah, yes: the philosophy, and their music . . ."

"No, the cars."

In the evening, by my bed, I light a candle for the icon of Seraphim of Sarov that I carry with me everywhere. And I write on a piece of paper, which I place before the image, this passage written by Jünger and dated December 1968: "In the sky, clouds were passing in front of the livid moon around which, at that moment, an American crew was orbiting. When I place a candle on a tomb, it has no effect, but its message is a rich one. It burns for the entire universe, confirming its meaning. If the astronauts circle the moon, the effect will be considerable, but the meaning of less account."

Next, to reward myself for having sent a sign to the Universe, I down two and a half liters of beer. This relaxes my legs no end.

MARCH 13

I had a clutter of weird dreams last night. Never happens in Paris. The standard explanation would hinge on the quality of my sleep, conducive to hallucinatory fantasizing. I tend toward the idea that the genius loci visits me secretly at night and, shining softly into the arcana of my psyche, shapes the substance of my dreams.

At dawn, a car from Irkutsk brings good old Yura, the pale-eyed fisherman who visited me not so long ago. He lives in a small log cabin at the station of Pokoyniki. He lives by fishing and helps Sergei with the more demanding chores. He has just spent two days in Irkutsk renewing his papers, stolen during the collapse of the Soviet Union.

"For three presidents, I hadn't left the woods: Yeltsin, Putin, and Medvedev!"

"What struck you the most in Irkutsk?"

"The stores! They've got everything. And it's so clean!"

"What else?"

"The people: they're speaking nicely to one another."

At noon, farewells to Yura, Sergei, and Natasha. I'll be home in three days. To the north of Pokoyniki Bay lies a frozen swamp; in winter one can take a certain revenge on terrain that in summer demands herculean efforts.

I retrace my steps. An evening halt at the cabin of Bolshoi Solontsovi. The stove takes a long time to start drawing. The cabin heats up slowly and I stay by the fire. Cats have figured everything out. Must remember to check, when I get back to France, if a "psychoanalysis of the cabin" has been published or not, because this evening, I feel as comfy as a fetus.

In the beginning, there was the organic womb, where life put itself together. In the marshes, coal beds, and peat bogs, bacteria macerated, and from the primordial soup would spring more complex life forms. Then the Earth delegated the task of maintaining warmth: uteruses, marsupial pouches, eggs provided their hothouse environment, while primitive habitats in turn acted as incubators. Men lived in caves, in the very womb of the Earth. Later, round igloos and yurts, wooden cabins and woolen tents were our homes. In the Siberian forest, the hermit expends a huge amount of energy on heating his shelter, the guarantee of bodily security and well-being. Only then is the solitary woodsman free to roam the forests and climb mountains despite the cold and other privations. He knows that his haven awaits him. The cabin fulfils the maternal function. The danger comes from constantly craving the comfort of this lair and vegetating there in a kind of semihibernation. This temptation threatens many Siberians, who can no longer manage to leave their cabins, where they regress to an embryonic state and replace the amniotic fluid with vodka.

MARCH 14

It's nice out today: 0°F. I knock off twelve and a half miles. Lava and ice are magical elements. Both have undergone the metamorphic influence of another element: cold air freezes water, fiery temperatures produce molten rock—and both will be transformed again when warm air melts the ice and cold water petrifies the lava. Walking on a frozen surface is not a trifling thing. Our footsteps land atop something in the making. Ice is one of the alchemical wonders of our world.

I'm a little more than six miles from Zavorotni, drag-
ging my sled northward, when a snowmobile catches up
with me and the driver cuts the engine. He and his passen-
ger seem numb with cold. Mika and Natalia own one of the
izbas at Zavorotni; they saw me from way off and headed for
my silhouette advancing along the coast. Within seconds,
Natalia spreads out a blanket on the black linoleum of the
lake and sets out cognac, a fish pie, and a thermos of coffee.
We stretch out around this bounty. Russians have a genius for
instantly producing the setting for a feast. How many times
have I run into them, these muzhiks who hail me from the
roadside? Gesturing, they invite me to sit down. In these situ-
ations, the new companions inevitably lean back onto their
elbows, with legs crossed and furry *shapkas* pushed up on
their foreheads. Sometimes a fire pops up, items leap out of
bags, someone opens a bottle of vodka, there are bursts of
laughter, glasses are filled. We share a loaf of bread, slice the
rest of some elk liver. The conversation grows lively, addressing essentially three subjects: the current weather, the state
of the track and terrain, the relative value of various modes
of transport. Occasionally someone touches on the theme of
the city, and everyone agrees: you have to be nuts to live cheek
by jowl like that. But out here, where there had been nothing, an oasis has sprung up within the borders of the blanket, and the secret of such transmutations is known only to
peoples of nomadic blood. Perov has painted such a scene
in his celebrated *Hunters at Rest*, 1871.[7] We see three shabby
men lounging on the ground; in front of them lie the ducks
and rabbit they have just bagged. One of the hunters is smoking, and they're all laughing as they chat about life. The light
is soft, the grass velvety. This painting fascinates me: it says

nothing about hope. It's a snapshot of immediate happiness. The sky could fall and the three friends wouldn't give a damn: they're sitting there, on the grass, lords of all they survey. Like the three of us on the ice.

Natalia and Mika roar off again. We've taken the time to empty the small bottle of cognac in seven toasts. The sun is already setting as I struggle on toward Zavorotni. With my habits, I would have been better off living on the eastern shore of Baikal, where the sun rises later and the afternoons last longer.

MARCH 15

I have thirteen and a half miles to go across the lake to reach home. As I'm preparing to leave Zavorotni, a squad of 4WDs appears on the horizon, their emergency roof lights flashing. Taking advantage of the statute exempting Zavorotni from the preserve regulations, V.M., a businessman from Irkutsk, is constructing an *izba* in the enclave. He'll use the place for country parties and invite his friends or clients out next year to fish, drink, and shoot at animals. This morning he has come with his entourage to inspect the work site. Sergei and Yura are with him. The General, as he is called here, distributes his largesse to the guardians of the preserve. In front of the slope where the foundations of the large *izba* are rising, there's a mob scene out on the ice. Everyone is drunk. Crates are being unloaded. One of V.M.'s lieutenants shows me his Saiga MK 7.62, which he always keeps handy to be ready if the fascists or the Yellow Peril show up on the ice. This is why Russian newspapers are full of stories about outings like these that go wrong. In Afghanistan, the Americans provide a finale for village festivities by shelling guests who celebrate by shooting into the air; Russians just shoot themselves up on their own.

A troop of drunken men, military weaponry, vodka, big vehicles, and technology: a recipe for death. Yura watches the goings-on with weary resignation. A malignant energy is gathering in the bay; all Russia is here in miniature: the dangerous overlords, the faithful Tolstoyan servant, Sergei the woodsman. And the humble attendants, knowing what profit they will reap from hanging around the powerful, swallow their disgust. This country in which the bonds of vassalage still survive was the laboratory of communism. I long for one thing only: to get back to my desert.

V.M. offers to drive me home in his Mercedes. I climb into the enormous car with Sergei and two other Russians, one of whom falls instantly asleep, while the other shouts into a walkie-talkie for three minutes before realizing that the thing is dead. The radio spits out a rap song. Sergei doesn't say a word. Some patronage comes at a heavy cost.

We are now having a drink at my place. Pointing to the window, V.M. says: "I lived in the USA for a year; I don't like the Americans' mentality. This is what I want: liberty, anarchy, the lake." We have more drinks. In the end, these guys are touching. They've got the mugs of fellows who'd tear Chechens limb from limb, and they delicately share their crackers with the titmouse. They and I are staying by this lake for the same reason, but in different ways. When they leave, I can breathe again. They have turned on the emergency light atop the Mercedes, in case they hit a traffic jam.

Silence comes back to me, the immense silence that is not the absence of sound but the disappearance of any interlocutor. I feel love welling inside me for these woods harboring deer, this lake gorged with fish, this sky criss-crossed by birds, and the intensity of my great beatnik love is proportional to the increasing distance between V.M.'s gang and my cabin. As they disappear, so does everything I fear: noise, the herd mentality, the urge to hunt—in short, the fever of the human mob.

I'm drunk and I need water. In the ten days I've been gone, my water holes have frozen over. I attack the lake with the ice ax, spending an hour and a half chopping out a handsome basin a yard wide and four feet deep. Water gushes up suddenly, and I dip into it with pleasure. This feeling of having *earned* one's water. My arm muscles ache. Once upon a time, in the fields and forests, living kept us in shape.

MARCH 16

In the world I left, the presence of others has some control over our actions and maintains discipline. In the city, when shielded from the eyes of our neighbors, we behave less elegantly. Who has never eaten alone, standing in the kitchen, happy not to have to set the table, eagerly devouring a can of cold ravioli? In a cabin, standards are always at risk of slipping. How many solitary Siberians, delivered from all social imperatives, knowing that there is no one to judge them, wind up flopped on a bed of cigarette butts, scratching their rashes? Crusoe was aware of this danger and decided, so as not to debase himself, to have supper every evening at a table and properly dressed, as if he had invited a guest.

Our fellow men confirm the reality of the world. If you close your eyes in the city, what a relief it is that reality doesn't erase itself: others can still perceive it! The hermit is alone in the face of nature. As the sole consciousness contemplating reality, he bears the burden of the representation of the world, its revelation before the human gaze.

Boredom doesn't frighten me in the least. There are worse pangs: the sorrow of not sharing with a loved one the beauty of lived moments. Solitude: what others miss out on by not being with the person who experiences it.

In Paris, I was warned before I left. Boredom would be my deadly enemy! I'd die of it! I listened politely. People who said such things assumed that they themselves were a superb form of entertainment. "Reduced to myself alone, I feed, it is true, on my own substance, but it does not run out. . . ," writes Rousseau in the *Reveries*.

Rousseau becomes aware of the challenge and ordeal of loneliness in the Fifth Walk. The solitary man must strictly devote himself to virtue, he says, and must never indulge in cruelty. If he behaves badly, the experience of his hermit's way of life will impose a double penance on him: on the one hand, he will have to endure an atmosphere corrupted by his own baseness, and on the other, he'll be forced to admit his own failure as a human being. In opposition to the natural man stands the civil man: "The civil man desires the approval of others; the solitary man must of necessity be content with himself, or his life is unbearable. And so the latter is forced to be virtuous." Rousseau's solitude generates goodness, and through a feedback effect, it will dissolve the memory of human wickedness. Solitude is the balm applied to the wound caused by the distrust of one's fellow men: "I would rather flee them than hate them," he writes in the Sixth Walk.

It is in the interest of the solitary man to treat his surroundings well, to rally to his cause all animals, plants, and gods. Why should he increase the austerity of his state with the hostility of the world? The hermit refuses to brutalize his environment. It's the Saint Francis of Assisi syndrome. The saint speaks to his brothers the birds, Buddha soothes the mad elephant with a gentle pat, Saint Seraphim feeds the bears, and Rousseau seeks consolation by botanizing.

At noon, I study the snow falling on the cedars. I try to let the sight sink into me so that I can follow the paths of as many snowflakes as possible. An exhausting exercise. And some people call this laziness!

This evening, the snow is still falling. Watching it, the Buddhist says, "Let's not expect any change"; the Christian, "Tomorrow will be better"; the pagan, "What does all this mean?"; the Stoic, "We'll see what happens"; the nihilist, "Let it bury everything"; and I say, "I'll have to cut some wood before the woodpile gets snowed under." Then I put another log in the stove and go to bed.

MARCH 17

Questions to clarify over the coming months:

Will I be able to stand myself?

Will I, at the age of thirty-seven, be able to change?

Why don't I miss anything I left behind?

The sky is still churning out snow. A morning at the window. In a cabin, life revolves around three activities.

1. The surveillance and profound understanding of one's field of vision (determined by the window frame). Nothing must go unnoticed.
2. Good housekeeping.

3. The welcoming of rare visitors, entertainment, the giving of directions and sometimes, on the contrary, the barring of the door to pests.

If I wanted to flatter myself, I'd say that these tasks make me something of a sentinel and my cabin a lookout post for the empire of trees. Actually, I'm a concierge and the cabin is my loge. Next time I head off to the woods, perhaps I'll hang out a sign that says Back Soon.

Toward evening, the slanting sunlight gives the snow a steely glint. The flat white tints now gleam like mercury. I try to take a photo of this phenomenon, but the image catches nothing of its brilliance. The vanity of photos. The frame reduces the real to its Euclidian value, killing the substance of things, compressing their flesh. Reality gets squashed against the screen. A world obsessed with images can't taste the mysterious emanations of life. No photographic lens will capture the memories unfolded by a landscape in our hearts. And what a face sends us in the way of negative ions or impalpable invitations—what camera could show them to us?

MARCH 18

My provisions are getting low. I have to figure out a way to fish. At Baikal the Siberians use a simple method: they dump a handful of what they call *bormash*, living water fleas collected in the marshes, through a hole in the ice. Attracted by this manna, fish gather at the hole, and the fisherman need only toss in his line. Having neither marshes nor *bormash* at hand, I borrow an old technique from the foresters: cutting quite a large hole in the ice fairly close to shore, where the lake is nine feet deep, I pile in cut cedar boughs and leave them to soak. In a few days, thousands of tiny organisms will have collected around the needles, ready to be harvested and used for bait.

The wind, still southerly, still smells like snow. The whiteness absorbs all sound. A rare silence reigns, and the air is pleasant. The thermometer shows 5° F.

MARCH 19

Last night, the cracking and booming woke me up. A colossal blow stronger than the rest shook the rafters of the cabin. Rebelling against its incarceration, the mass of water is banging on the lid.

Still snowing. More stillness. Before, I was traveling around like an arrow from a bow; now I'm a stake driven into the ground. And I'm vegetalizing. My being is taking root. I'm slowing down, drinking lots of tea, becoming hypersensitive to variations in the light. I'm not eating meat anymore. My cabin: a hothouse.

INTERIOR WORLD	EXTERIOR WORLD
Maternal cabin	Paternal lake
Heat	Cold, dryness
Softness of wood	Hardness of ice
Safety	Constant danger
Purring of the stove	Cracking, booming
Tears of resin on the beams	Sparkling of the ice
Intellectual labor	Physical labor
The body fattens	The body dries out
The skin grows pale	The skin weathers and chaps

Spent a long time on firewood duty. Another tree cut down and up and stacked away. Then I cut paths with a shovel through the snow to the lakeshore, the *banya*, and the wood-pile. Tolstoy recommended working four hours a day to earn the right to shelter and sustenance.

Tonight, insomnia. I imagine the animals prowling or sleeping near the cabin at this moment. Minks no one wants to turn into coats, deer no one dreams of baking into pâtés, bears no one wants to kill to prove his virility.

MARCH 20

These days, titmice tap at the window every morning. Their beaks sound my wake-up alarm. Mild weather; I set out a stool a mile or so from the shore and smoke a Romeo y Julieta no. 2 (a bit dry) while admiring the view. The mountains, until now, have been something I've learned to climb, descend, navigate, and survey. I have not yet ever *looked* at them.

In the evening, Casanova. Locked up in Venice "under the Leads," a small prison in the Doge's palace for detainees of high status and named for the lead plates on the roof, Casanova writes: "Believe that in order to be free, you need only believe that you are." His liking for sugar-coated candies filled with a powder made from the beloved's hair. (I should have brought some of those with me.) His critique, made to Voltaire, of human utopias: "Your premier passion is the love of humanity... but you can only love it as it is. It does not deserve the blessings you would bestow upon it. ... I have never laughed so heartily as at Don Quixote having a hard time defending himself from the galley slaves he has just generously set free."

MARCH 21

Today is the first day of spring. Blue sky above and I'm heading into the woods. I climb up along a frozen river running down to the lake; it's about a third of a mile north of my cabin.

Nature's solitude meets mine. And our two solitudes confirm their existence. Laboring through the powder snow, I recall Michel Tournier's meditation on the joy of having a companion at one's side—to convince oneself that the world does exist. I'm the only person looking at these ash trees with their vertically striped bark. The shrubs are hung with clumps of snow like Christmas ornaments, and the tortured silhouettes of larches make the valley seem like an etching; in Chinese drawings it always looks as though the rivers and mountains were suffering. The human gaze is a baptism, but at present, no one is helping mine to give life to these forms. I have only my field of vision to make the world *appear*. If there were two of us, we'd conjure up more things.

I make progress, I'm past the grove; it's now out of sight. Does it still exist? If I had someone with me, I'd ask my companion to make sure the world doesn't disappear behind me. Schopenhauer's affirmation that the world exists only as the representation of the subject is an amusing view of the mind, but it's claptrap. This forest—don't I feel it radiating with all its strength behind my back?

When the valley grows tighter, at about 2,600 feet, I reach the summit of the sharp ridge. Ye gods of the slopes! What a struggle to climb 650 feet through this morass of dwarf pines buried in snow! A bright line snakes through the greenish bronze mass of the taiga: it's the ash trees with their blond branches, marking out the torrent's course with a stream of honey.

I hike down again in two hours through long white alleys, empty esplanades, and silent avenues. The forest in winter is a dead city. In the cabin, I plunge back into Casanova. After his visit to an important pilgrimage site, the Abbey of Einsiedeln in Switzerland: "I felt that to be happy, I needed nothing more than a library." Apropos of a young Italian woman: "I felt mortified at having to leave her without having paid to her charms the principal homage they deserved." During Casanova's travels, he stays in Rome, Paris, Munich, Geneva, Venice, and Naples. He speaks French, English, Italian, and Latin. He meets Voltaire, Hume, and Goldoni. He quotes Copernicus, Ariosto, and Horace. His lovers are named Donna Lucrezia, Hedwige, or Henriette. Two centuries later, technocrats announce that we must urgently "build Europe."

At eight o'clock, I set my table. Tonight: soup, some pasta, Tabasco sauce, tea, eight or nine ounces of vodka, and a Partagás Cuban in a tube. The Tabasco allows you to swallow anything at all with the impression that you're actually eating something. Before going to sleep, I light a wax taper in front of the picture of my darling and smoke while watching the flame flicker over her face. Why do separated lovers complain? For consolation, they need only believe in the incarnation of being in the icon. I blow out the oil lamps and go to bed.

Today I have not harmed any living creatures on this planet. *Do no harm.* It's strange that the desert anchorites never offer this beautiful concern among the explanations for their retreat. St. Pachomius (the founder of Christian cenobitic monasticism), St. Anthony, the Abbé de Rancé—these men speak of their hatred for their centuries, their battles with demons, their inner torment, their thirst for purity, their impatience to enter the Heavenly Realm—but never of the idea of living without harming anyone. *No harm done.* After a day in the cabin of North Cedar Cape, that's what a man can tell himself when he looks in the mirror.

MARCH 22

A stormy night. The Russians call the wind roaring down the western mountainsides of Baikal the *sarma.*[8] The clanking of the tools hanging underneath the eaves kept me awake for hours. How can the birds stay in their nests? Will they still be here, alive, tomorrow?

The wind has blasted the snow from the lake surface and given the ice back to me. I skate for two hours beneath a chilly sun, listening to Maria Callas.

This evening, because I've nothing much to do after having brought in enough wood for five days, I jot down the reasons for my retreat.

REASONS WHY I'M LIVING ALONE IN A CABIN

I talked too much.

I wanted silence.

Too behind with my mail and too many people to see.

I was jealous of Crusoe.

It's better heated than my place in Paris.

Tired of running errands.

So I can scream and live naked.

Because I hate the telephone and traffic noise.

MARCH 23

I snowshoe along the lakeshore and through the woods all day long. This idea that landscapes have a memory. An agricultural plain remembers the ringing of the Angelus bell. A meadow full of poppies remembers the puppy loves of childhood. But here? The forests have no memories. They are without transformation, without History; they say nothing, and no echo of human actions lingers beneath their foliage. The taiga spreads over the land for itself alone. It covers slopes, storms up to peaks without owing anyone anything. Man finds nature's indifference toward him hard to bear. The sight of a virgin forest gives him dreams of germination and production. Where man's gaze falls upon the taiga, his ax soon falls in turn. Ah, the anguish of industrious creatures who suddenly realize that the wilderness does very well without them...Who loves nature for its intrinsic value and not for its gifts? In *The Roots of Heaven,* Romain Gary presents a concentration-camp prisoner who holds up better than his companions: lying in his bunk at night, he closes his eyes and pictures herds of wild elephants. Knowing that out there on the savannas these mighty beasts range free is enough to put steel in his soul. Thinking about the pachyderms gives him strength. And as long as there are taigas empty of man, I'll feel good. There is consolation in wildness.

I climb to the very top of the rise and build a big fire up there, in the shelter of a granite boulder. Cooking some soup gives me an excuse to sit quietly looking at the cadaverous face of the lake, with its blue and purple blotches, its marbling, its patches and lichens.

MARCH 24

I don't dare get up this morning. My will is roaming freely in the field of blank days. The danger: remaining paralyzed until nightfall, staring at the whiteness thinking, *God, how free I am!*

It's snowing again. There's no one. Not even a vehicle in the distance. The only thing passing here is time. The happiness in my life at seeing the titmice appear... Never again will I make fun of those old ladies who cherish a canary at the center of their lives or coo over their poodles with baby-talk on the posh sidewalks of Auteuil. Or those old men in the Tuileries carefully feeding pigeons with the birdseed they clutch in little paper bags. Hanging out with animals makes one young.

Lady Chatterley. In chapter 7, Clifford, no question, is a suffocating presence, he disgusts poor little Constance: "... he talked, always talked; infinite small analysis of people and motives, and results, characters and personalities, till now she had had enough. For years she had loved it, until she had enough, and then suddenly it was too much. She was thankful to be alone." I close the book, go outside, dig the ax out of the snow and for two hours, whack away like a madman at the chopping-block, galvanized by Lady Constance. There's more truth in the blows of my ax and the cackling of the jays than in droning psychological explications. "What must first be proved is worth little." (Nietzsche in the *Twilight*.) Letting life express itself through blood, snow, the cutting edge of the ax, and the gleam of sunshine on a chattering rook.

Today, out in the snow, I retrieve my *bormash* trap, delicately breaking the ice to avoid disturbing the boughs. I spread out a blanket, lift up the branches, and shake them over a bucket. Thousands of organisms quiver in the clear water. I pour them into a bottle—and I have my bait. In a few days, I'll go fishing.

You have to have a warped mind to think *Lady Chatterley's Lover* is an erotic novel. The book is a requiem for wounded nature. The England of peaceful woods and pastures, of leafy glades full of memories, is dying before the heroine's eyes. Mining is ravaging British soil. The pits are gutting the land; the smokestacks rise into smudged and gritty skies. The air stinks, soot stains the brick buildings; even men's faces are growing hard. The country is prostituting itself to industry, and a new race of businessmen-technicians expounds abstract sociopolitical themes and speculates about technology. It's the death-agony of the world. "The industrial England blots out the agricultural England." Constance feels the sap rise in her flesh; she understands that progress desubstantializes the world. Lawrence puts prophetic words into the young woman's mouth as she protests against the uglification of the countryside, the debasement of the human spirit, the tragedy of a people losing its vitality ("its manhood," she says) in the drumbeat of mechanization. Primitive and pagan love blossoms within Lady Chatterley at the same time as she witnesses the shipwreck of the modern soul, sucked into a sinister energy: a Promethean "madness" weakens humanity in the din of the machine. In his *Confession*, Gorky stakes out the opposing position: as a revolutionary, he rejoices in Russia's immense dedication to progress, and he predicts that the monstrous energy concentrated in industrial centers will spread throughout the world in a magnetic cloud. This psychophysiological force will persuade all the peoples of the Earth to roll up their sleeves to make every tomorrow sing. Lawrence was anxious about the titanic nervous tension roiling the world. Gorki hailed it with all his heart. Lawrence knew that the sweet peacefulness of the countryside is one face of its beauty. Gorki believed only in the splendor of skies crackling from the metallurgy of iron and steel. And Constance, sweating with desire, suffering the Passion of the Earth, cries out beneath the sheltering boughs of the forest like a tragic actress—whose lament has already been drowned out by the clatter of machines: "Ah God, what has man done to man?"

This evening, I contemplate the lake, sitting on my wooden bench beneath the canopy of cedars. This above all: a lovely landscape before one's eyes. Then everything can fall into place; life may begin. Lady Chatterley is right. And I'd be delighted to welcome her here for a few days, I tell myself, before going off to bed.

MARCH 25

Up with the sun. Faced with such glory, I go back to bed for a bit. This morning the weather allows me to go outside for the first time in days. I climb up to the waterfall by a different route, along the right bank of the torrent. The forest awaits, clotted with snow: my real test. Two hours to get through a quarter mile of uneven terrain. Woodpeckers hammer at the dead trees. Then I have an eighth of a mile of good hard footing. After that, the ordeal of crossing a deep, narrow valley full of dwarf pines. I tumble into pitfalls three feet deep. I'm aiming for a granite ledge a little over three hundred feet above the iced-over waterfall. From below, with my binoculars, I think I see a platform suitable for a bivouac.

Fine snow is blurring my vision of the lake lying placidly at the foot of the mountain. My intuition was good: at an altitude of 3,610 feet, the rocky ridge offers a perfect shelf, a spectacular observation post. A wonderful place for an idyllic night of love. I've got the venue, anyway; that's already something.

I slog down from there in snow up to my thighs, panting like a real Russian; then I keep quiet, so I can hear the snow crinkling on the backs of the white trees.

At the mouth of the river, I limber up my muscles on the flat ground near the lake by following the tracks of a fox, which walked almost two miles out onto the ice and looped around to come back. Simply a fox going for a stroll.

The snow is coming down hard now. This masking of the world makes the bite of solitude ten times more sharp. What is solitude? A companion for all seasons.

It's a salve for wounds. It's an echo chamber in which impressions are magnified when you are the only one arousing them. It imposes responsibility: I am the ambassador of the human race in a forest devoid of men. I must enjoy this sight on behalf of those who are deprived of it. Solitude fosters thought, for the only conversation possible is with oneself. It sweeps away all chitchat, allowing the sounding of one's self. It calls to mind the memory of those we love. It binds the hermit in friendship with plants and beasts and perhaps a little god just happening by.

At the end of the afternoon, I check on my *bormash*: the tiny creatures are swimming around in the bottle. Tomorrow or the next day, they'll be bait.

It's eight in the evening. I'm resting in my cube, at the edge of the forest, at the foot of the mountain, along the edge of the lake, in the love of everything around me.

I fall asleep reading Chinese poetry. I learn by heart a verse to offer in a conversation after running out of arguments:

"There is deep significance in all this. Just as I was about to say so, I'd already forgotten what I was going to say."

MARCH 26

Snow. I walk on the lake and hold out my face, mouth open. I drink in snowflakes at the breast of the sky.

In the evening, I cut a hole in the ice with the hand-drill, in thirteen feet of water and a cable's length from shore. The cloud of crustaceans turns the water murky. Now I need only await the arrival of the spotted char. I'm getting tired of pasta al Tabasco.

MARCH 27

A morning of Chinese poetry. I arrived here with snow-shoes, ice skates, crampons, an ice ax, and fishing line, and I find myself reading stories in which hermits sitting on stone benches watch the wind flutter through bamboo groves. Ah, the genius of the Chinese! Inventing the principle of "non-action" to justify staying all day in the golden light of Yunnan on the threshold of a cabin....

Fishing in the evening. I'm perched on my stool, moving my hook up and down. Through the hole I can see char passing by, attracted by the *bormash*. Fishing is a Chinese activity: one opens oneself to the flow of hours while staring at the pole, hoping it will twitch. Which doesn't happen once the whole evening.

I drown my sorrow at returning empty-handed in eight or nine shots of vodka and let the alcohol do its work.

Chinese poets! I need some help here!

MARCH 28

Strange, this need for transcendence. Why believe in a God outside his own creation? The crackling of the ice, the gentleness of the titmice, and the puissance of the mountains stir me more than any idea of the master of these ceremonies. They are enough for me. If I were God, I would atomize myself into billions of facets so I could dwell in ice crystals, cedar needles, the sweat of women, the scales of spotted char, and the eyes of the lynx. More exhilarating than floating about in infinite space, watching from afar as the blue planet self-destructs.

Dense fog has settled onto the lake. The horizon is gone. I bundle up and head out across Baikal. After about a mile, I can't see the shore behind me. I walk for two hours. Only my footsteps link me to the cabin. I've brought along neither compass nor GPS, and if the wind comes up, erasing my tracks, I'll lose my way. I don't know what pushes me on. Some slightly morbid force. I plunge into nothingness. Abruptly, after two hours, I say, "That's enough" and turn back, lengthening my stride. In two hours I see the mountain appear behind the white veil, and I reach the cabin.

There is a Chinese tradition in which old men would retire to a cabin to die. Some of them had served the emperor, held government posts, while others were scholars, poets, or simple hermits. Their cabins were all alike, the settings selected according to strict criteria. The hut had to be on a mountain, near a source of water, with a bush for the wind to caress. Sometimes the view was toward a valley alive with the bustle of humanity. Incense smoke helped time to pass. In the evening, a friend would appear, to be welcomed with a glass of tea and a few circumspect words. After having wanted to act upon the world, these men retrenched, determined to let the world act upon them. Life is an oscillation between two temptations.

But please note! Chinese non-action is not acedia. Non-action sharpens all perception. The hermit absorbs the universe, paying acute attention to its smallest manifestation. Sitting cross-legged beneath an almond tree, he hears the shock of a petal striking the surface of a pond. He sees the edge of a feather vibrate as a crane flies overhead. He feels the perfume of a happy flower rise from the blossom to envelop the evening.

And this evening, I'm learning the funeral oration of Tao Yuanming, who died in 427: "Dignified in my humble hut, at my ease I drink wine and compose poems, attuned to the course of things, conscious of my destiny, now free, therefore, from all mental reservations. . . ." [9]

I go to bed thinking there's no point in keeping a journal when others can sum up their lives in thirty words!

MARCH 29

This morning: 27°F. First springlike day. The titmice are flocking beneath the southern window. Suddenly, gusts shake the cedars and snow falls. The landscape is striped with gray gossamer.

I read Chinese verses while sipping vodka. If the world collapsed, would I hear any echo? A cabin is a wooden bunker. The logs are such a handsome protective barrier! The pine beams, alcohol, and poetry form a triple carapace. "My cabin is far away and me, I know nothing": a Russian proverb born in the taiga.

Poles apart are the diktats of Paris: "You will answer the telephone! You will be reachable at all times! You will have an opinion on everything! You will be indignant!"

The Cabin Credo: Do not react . . . never let your buttons be pushed . . . never give up . . . float slightly tipsy in the snowy silence . . . admit indifference to the fate of the world . . . and read Chinese writers.

The wind strengthens. The world bangs on the window-pane to be let in. Defend me, my books! Protect me, my bottle! Shield me, my cabin, from this northeast wind determined to distract me. If someone brought me a newspaper hot off the press right now, I'd take it for an earthquake.

I was almost certain they'd turn up: I happen across these verses by Du Mu, a ninth-century poet.[10]

> *The small pavilion can barely fit a bed in lengthwise*
> *pouring myself drinks all day I watch the mountains*
> *admirable when in the night the wind flies in with rain*
> *amid drunkenness the noise knocks on the window pane*
> > *in vain.*

MARCH 30

I hotfooted it up to the ice waterfall today via a new route. I take the first valley to the south of my cabin, and at 3,280 feet, I begin working my way all around the shoulder. I pass the ridge and a few sentinels of rotten granite looming up through the snow. I continue along the flank of the slope on the hard snow, occasionally tripped up by a stretch of dwarf pines. It takes me five whole hours of hard labor to reach the left bank of the notch cradling the ice waterfall. My secret hope, in staying so long above the tree line, is to catch sight of a deer, but aside from some wolverine tracks disappearing into the woods, which fill me with joy, there is nothing.

Back at the lake, I catch my first fish at five o'clock, a second one three minutes later, and a third an hour and a half after that. Three quicksilver char, electric with fury, gleam on the ice. The skin is shot through with quivers of energy. I kill them and look out at the plain, murmuring the words of thanks Siberians once addressed to the animal they had destroyed or the world they had just made a little poorer. In modern society, the carbon tax has replaced this "Thank you, I'm sorry."

The happiness of having on your plate the fish you've caught, with a glass of water you've fetched, and the wood you've chopped in the stove: the hermit goes to the source. The flesh, water, and wood are still fresh.

I remember my days in the city. I'd go down to shop for supper and wander along the aisles of a supermarket, glumly tossing items into my cart. We've become the hunter-gatherers of a denatured, unnatural world.

The urban liberal, leftist, revolutionary, and upper-middle-class citizen all pay money for bread, gas, and taxes. The hermit asks nothing from the state and gives nothing to the state. He disappears into the woods and thrives there. His retreat constitutes a *loss of income* for the government. Becoming a loss of income should be the objective of true revolutionaries. A repast of grilled fish and blueberries gathered in the forest is more antistatist than a protest demonstration bristling with black flags. Those who dynamite the citadel need the citadel. They are against the state in the sense that they lean against it. Walt Whitman: "I have nothing to do with this system, not even enough to oppose it." On that October day five years ago when I discovered old Walt's *Leaves of Grass*, I had no idea that reading it would lead me to a cabin. It's dangerous to open a book.

A retreat is a revolt. Entering one's cabin means vanishing from surveillance screens. The hermit erases himself. He sends no more numeric traces, no telephonic signals, no banking data. He divests himself of all identity. He effects a kind of reverse hacking, and leaves the Great Game. No need, moreover, to head for the woods. Revolutionary asceticism can adapt to an urban milieu. The consumer society offers the *choice* to conform to it, and with a little discipline... Surrounded by abundance, some are free to live like pushovers but others may play the monk and stay lean amid the murmur of books, retreating to inner forests without leaving their apartments. In a society of penury, there is no other alternative. One is condemned to a state of want and conditioned by it. Willpower is neither here nor there. A famous Soviet joke says a guy goes into a butcher shop and asks, "You have any bread?" Answer: "Ah, no, this is the place where we have no meat, so for the place where they have no bread, go next door to the bakery." The Hungarian lady who raised me taught me such things, and I often think of her. *The consumer society* is a somewhat vile expression, born of the phantasm of childish grownups disappointed at having been too spoiled. They haven't the strength to reform on their own and dream of being constrained to live in sober moderation.

At seven this evening, I attempt to make myself blini with my stash of flour kept in watertight bags. An hour later, I place on my wooden plank a single charred pancake. I spend a half-hour outside until the smoke is gone from the cabin, then open a packet of Chinese noodles.

MARCH 31

For a few days now, I've been conducting a Pavlovian experiment that is beginning to bear fruit. At nine in the morning, I play a tune on my flute at the window before tossing some crumbs to the titmice. This morning they arrived at the first notes, well before I'd set out their ration. I breathe deeply of the dawn air, surrounded by birds. The only thing missing is Snow White.

A day up in the heights. I head back up the "white valley," a large combe filled with Japanese larches to the north of my cabin. After five hours of struggle in the deep snow, I reach 5,250 feet. Sometimes I feel like a moose stuck up to the chest in glue. I think I'm about 980 feet from the summit, but it's very cold and getting late. I head down to North Cedar Cape. Some lynx tracks cross my own. The animal must have passed by one or two hours earlier and still be somewhere in the vicinity. I bend down to sniff the paw prints but can't smell a thing. I feel less alone. There were two of us traipsing around the neighborhood today.

This evening, I split some wood in the clearing. First you must put the cleaving ax deep into the wood with a powerful blow. Once the metal is deeply set, you raise the ax and the log it's stuck in—and whack the whole thing with all your strength down on the chopping block. If the blow is well struck, the log splits in two. Then all you have to do is lop off smaller pieces with a hatchet. My aim is true; I'm no longer missing my target. A month ago, it took me three times as long to prepare the necessary firewood. In a few weeks, I'll be a chopping machine. When the metal strikes exactly where it should and the logs split with a ripping sound, I convince myself that cutting wood is a martial art.

APRIL

✝✝✝✝✝✝✝✝✝✝✝✝✝✝✝✝✝✝✝✝✝✝✝✝✝✝✝✝✝✝✝✝✝✝✝✝

The Lake

APRIL 1

It's nine in the morning. I'm reading Michel Déon's novel about a man who withdraws to the Irish countryside, where the people are passing strange, when I come upon these words: "But you know, in spite of all my willpower, solitude is the most difficult thing to protect"—and my door flies violently open. Displaying typically Russian energy, four fishermen burst into the cabin without warning, as if they intended to beat me senseless.

They bellow exuberant greetings. They're driving to Severobaikalsk, a large town on the northern end of Lake Baikal, to sell the fish they've caught in the southern sector of the preserve. I hadn't heard their truck engine and in my fright have spilled my tea all over *Un taxi mauve*. There's Sasha, who's missing some fingers; my old acquaintance Igor (also missing some digits), whom I met five years ago out on the ice; Volodya T., whose former cabin I now inhabit; and Andrei, a Buryat I've never seen before. I perform the ritual: slice up the sausage they've placed on the table, open a bottle, bring out the glasses. Two of my visitors abstain, but the rest of us set about getting drunk.

I ask each of them to tell me how he spent his military service. Volodya was in a tank in Mongolia (a toast to tank crews); Sasha was a radio operator on the shores of the Arctic Ocean (a toast to those Arctic shores); Igor was a sailor in

103

the Crimea (a toast to the fleet); and Andrei was a gunner in Cherkasy, in central Ukraine (a toast to the Russian politics of pacification in the Caucasus). The postings of Russian conscripts form a trans-Siberian journey to rival the one Blaise Cendrars described in a modernist poem about his Russian travels in 190. My camera is in position on the shelf, set in movie mode; I press the button. The conversation grows livelier, fueled by the bite of Kedrovaya vodka in a 104° F cabin.

TRANSCRIPTION OF THE CONVERSATION OF APRIL 1

SASHA: I say to myself, "Fucking hell!"

ME: What will be, will be.

SASHA: Brother drunks, alkies! (To Igor:) And you, not drinking? Bravo!

ANDREI: May everything go well! Everything, that means everything: love, family, everything.

ME: You're returning from where?

SASHA: From Cape Shartlai. There's this poor guy, he's out there dying. All winter long, he's been spending his time dying.

IGOR: No broad, no anyone! Alone.

SASHA: It's his boss's fault. He abandoned him out there for the winter without provisions!

ME: Who's his boss?

SASHA: It's that fuckhole... shithead... faggot... the hunter.

IGOR: The other day, I asked him, "You've got no cartridges for the gun?" So he says: "No. The wolves come up a few yards away. I throw stones to drive them off."

SASHA: When we went by Shartlai, we saw wolf tracks on the road.

ANDREI: Huge ones, big as this, and really fresh, fucking shit.

SASHA: And him, the guy, he goes out at four in the morning, he sees their eyes shining thirty feet away. "So?" I ask him. "Why didn't you shoot?" And he tells me, "Haven't got any cartridges." We went back to see him in January. His dog had croaked. It had had nothing to eat at all. The dog was chained up, it died of hunger. The puppies . . .

ANDREI: Looked like skeletons.

ME: And him, what's he eat?

SASHA: I don't know.

IGOR: I don't understand why no supplies are sent to him. I mean, what is this? A man going hungry in the forest!

SASHA: Shit. And all winter long trucks are going by, but no one stops and no one sends him any provisions.

IGOR: It's the first time I've seen that. A guy living completely alone like that. And no one gives a fuck. Even a dick wouldn't stay in his cunt of a hole.

SASHA: And yet he even seems happy!

ME: He's a slave.

SASHA: That's true, that's true! I didn't dare use that word: a slave.

VOLODYA: A serf, we also say in Russian.

ANDREI: Even a slave, you don't torture him like that.

IGOR: No.

SASHA: He's got a really bad boss. A shit boss. That's no boss.

ME: But he had no other choice. He couldn't have stayed in his village, with no work, no money. . . .

IGOR: But he's not getting any pay where he is, either.

SASHA: Maybe he's better off here. If he'd stayed back in his village . . .

IGOR: He'd have already died of alcoholism.

SASHA: Yes! He'd have already died of alcoholism.

IGOR: Well of course! Of course!

SASHA: Whereas now, at least he's still alive. . . .

IGOR: There you have it: alive.

VOLODYA: By the way, Sylvain, there's a crisis, seems that Europe's in a real bad way. Especially Greece: that place is on its knees. Done for. Fucked.

ME: Fucked?

IGOR: Fucked.

VOLODYA: You won't be able to go home anymore.

SASHA: It's Greece did that to you. Greece is in deep shit.

VOLODYA: Yup, in shit.

IGOR: Yes, it's a huge catastrophe!

VOLODYA: Fucking fucked up, and there's some revolts going on over there.

SASHA: Yes, revolts, people running around shouting!

IGOR: A democratic total mess.

SASHA: He's still happy that in 1812 our Cossacks taught the French how to wash themselves and scrub their necks. They never bathed before that. Can you imagine? In 1812, the Cossacks built them *banyas*. Historical fact. That's why the French invented perfumes, to cover up the nasty body odors and the bad smells of the cities. It stank all over, France! Our Cossacks who went there in 1812, they taught them to wash themselves in baths. I can assure you, it's true.

IGOR: Catastrophe! Nightmare! Guys: *catastrophe, cataclysm—* they're French words, Sylvain told me so.

SASHA: I'm not surprised.

VOLODYA: Fuck.

That's where the recording ends. The Russians make a few more toasts to weird stuff, and then suddenly they're shouting that they've got to "get the fucking hell going," and they put on their jackets, curse their gloves and their caps and their scarves, and one of them kicks the door, calling it a fucker, and, leaving me that good sausage barely half gone, off they go, and there I am on the shore, a little the worse for wear, looking at a day wrecked by vodka.

Every time Russian fishermen visit my cabin, I feel as if a cavalry division has come to bivouac in my kitchen garden. Fatalism, spontaneity, despotism: Mongol character traits have been injected into the Slavic venous system. The nomad shows through the woodsman. The dreadful Marquis de Custine, who wrote a celebrated account of his visit to Russia during the reign of Nicholas I, was right: Russia is "charged with conveying Asia to Europe." In consideration of which, I spend an hour setting my trashed cabin to rights.

APRIL 2

It was −4° F last night, and I finally got around to nailing strips of felt on the underside of the door. This morning I drank my tea while checking messages left on the window panes by the frost. Who could decipher them? Is there writing hidden in these things?

This evening, I at last make a success of my blini. Blini are like children: never take your eye off them. I invent blini stuffed with spotted char. First, catch a char. Cut wood. Make a fire. Cook the fish in the embers with some dill or fennel. Make the blini (with a few drops of beer if you have no yeast). Pull the flesh of the char to pieces over a blini. Put another blini atop that one. Wash the whole thing down with half a pint of vodka at room temperature.

I dine, gazing out the window. Some people can dine exclusively by feasting their eyes on a landscape. That is one definition of Eden. To live ensconced in a space one may encompass with a look, circumambulate in a day, and envision in the mind.

My dinners at Baikal contain a faint glimmer of *gray energy*, which is embodied energy. Gray energy skyrockets when the caloric value of the food is less than the energy necessarily expended in its production and transportation. The orange once offered at Christmas was a treasure. Everyone knew it was swollen with gray energy, and they appreciated the cost of its voyage. A catfish pulled from a bend in the Mekong by a Laotian fisherman and grilled on the riverbank has zero gray energy. Like my chars, cooked a few yards from the fishing hole. Steak from Argentina, however, from cattle who feed on soybeans on the estancias of the pampas before being shipped across the Atlantic to Europe, is tarred with the brush of infamy. Gray energy is the shadow of karma, the balance due for our sins. One day we will be called upon to pay it.

PARTIAL LIST OF A FEW HISTORIC

MEALS WITH LOW GRAY ENERGY

The manna from heaven that fell at the feet of the Jewish
    people.

The youths and maidens offered to the Minotaur by the
    Athenians.

The bread and wine at the Last Supper.

The loaves and fishes by the Sea of Galilee.

Pelops, the son of Tantalus.

The blood Tartar warriors sucked from their horses' necks
    on the open steppes.

The dried lizards Saint Pachomius dined on in the desert.

The Christian missionaries who sailed to the Malayo-
    Polynesian islands and wound up in cannibal cooking pots.

In spite of appearances, the bears killed by famished Ukrainians after the fall of the Soviet Union were full of gray energy: the beasts had been brought from Siberia and raised in captivity. Forty years ago, the survivors of a plane crash in the Andes ate the flesh of their dead companions. They consumed a high-gray-energy meal: the meat had been flown in to the site.

The nutrients of the lake and the forest enrich the blood of the fishermen of Baikal. The air, water, and humus of Siberia pulse through their arteries. In light of these biological findings, the rights of the soil should be taken into consideration. Because blood draws upon the substance of the soil, your identity would take root in the geographic space that nourishes you. If you partake of imported jams, you are a citizen of the world.

APRIL 3

I've begun Defoe's *Robinson Crusoe*, have finished Tournier's *Friday* and *An Island to Oneself*, Tom Neale's account of the six years he spent on the tiny deserted island of Anchorage in the atoll of Suwarrow.

One can establish certain traits characteristic of castaways, common similarities that outline the archetypical figure of the solitary survivor cast up on a shore.

A sense of injustice at the time of the shipwreck, followed
by curses directed at the gods, men, and sailing ships in
general.
The appearance of a slightly megalomaniacal syndrome: the
castaway convinces himself that he is a privileged being.

The feeling of being the lord of a realm and of ruling over all
animal, vegetable, and mineral subjects: "If I pleased,
I might call myself king, or emperor over the whole
country which I had possession of. There were no
rivals," says Defoe's Robinson.

The need to constantly confirm the merits of the solitary life
by insisting to oneself at every occasion on the beauty of
such an existence.

The contradictory wavering between the hope of prompt
rescue and revulsion at any contact with one's fellow
man.

Panic over the slightest intrusion of human beings on the
island.

Empathy with the natural world (this may take several years
to appear).

An insistence on strictly regulating varying periods of action,
meditation, and leisure.

The temptation to transform each moment of existence into
a staged game.

The slightly euphoric feeling of playing the role of an
observer or watchman on the margins of a humanity
gone astray.

The risk of contracting the *ivory tower syndrome*, which in
its extreme form leads the castaway to see himself both
as the repository of universal wisdom and the redeemer
of the sins of mankind.

APRIL 4

Today I read a lot, skated for three hours in a Viennese light while listening to the *Pastorale*, caught a char and harvested a pint of bait, looked out the window at the lake through the steam of my black tea, chopped up a tree trunk nine feet long and split two days of wood, cooked and ate some good kasha, and reflected that paradise was right there for the taking in the course of my day.

APRIL 5

Gusty weather last night. Northern winds thrashed the edge of the woods until noon. The thermometer says −9° F. What a delightful spring! When the afternoon turns mild, I begin building a table. Thick cedar branches for the legs, with a braced frame, and for the top, four planks that had been slumbering sheltered by the porch roof. Three hours of work, and by nightfall, I have my table. I take it down to the beach and set it out in the snow, where the clearing opens in front of the cedar shaped like a shell. Then I sit down on a log and lean back against the tree trunk. Those people who forbid you to put your feet on a table . . . do not understand the pride of a woodworker.

In the evening, I smoke a Partagás out in the cold, with my elbows on my new "observation deck." The table and I, we already love each other very much. On this Earth, it's good to lean on something.

This life brings peace. Not that all longings fade away. The cabin is no tree of Buddhist Enlightenment. A hermitage draws ambitions back to proportions of possibility. By restricting the panoply of actions, one goes deeper into each experience. Reading, writing, fishing, scaling heights, skating, strolling in the woods . . . Existence becomes reduced to a dozen or so activities. The castaway enjoys absolute freedom—but within the limits of his island. At the beginning of all Robinsonian narratives, the hero tries to escape by building a boat. He is convinced that anything is possible, that happiness lies just over the horizon. Cast up once again on the shore, he understands that he will not escape and, at peace, discovers that limitation brings joy. He is then said to *resign himself*. Resigned, the hermit? No more than the city dweller who, haggard, suddenly realizes beneath the twinkling lights of the boulevard that his whole life will still not be enough for him to sample all the attractions at the party.

APRIL 6

In the fourth century, in Upper Egypt, the shifting sand dunes of the Sahara in Wadi Natrun were swarming with monks in rags. The anchorites ran to the desert to follow in the footsteps of Saints Anthony and Pachomius. Their eyes gazed with an unhealthy light out of leathery faces. Reality horrified them: they found life degrading. Specters nourished on lizards, they rejected the world, fearing its savors. Their sensations were their enemies. If they dreamed of a pitcher of water, they believed Satan was tempting them. They wished to die to attain the other realm, the one guaranteed by Holy Scripture to be eternal.

The hermit of the taiga is a world away from such renunciation. The mystics tried to disappear from this earth. The woodsman wants to be reconciled with it. The ascetics waited for the advent of something not of this life, while the forester seeks the serendipitous appearance of brief pleasures, here and now. They wanted eternity; he craves the granting of prayers. They hoped to die; he desires felicity. They hated their bodies; he hones his senses. In short, if you want to have a good time around a bottle of vodka, you're better off running into a hermit in the woods rather than a holy fool perched on his pillar.

Out in those deserts, encountering one's fellow man was an event. The anchorites forgot what a human face looked like, and when a visitor appeared, many of them fell to their knees, convinced this apparition was a demon.

Which is what happens to me when Volodya T. pops in on me this morning, arriving in a jeep to collect some belongings. Why doesn't this damn door ever open to reveal a svelte Danish ski champion come to celebrate her twenty-third birthday on the shores of Baikal?

"A vodka?" I ask Volodya.

"No," he says.

"You're not drinking?"

"I stopped."

"When?"

"Twenty years ago, before I came here. One day I woke up and my wife and children were gone. Family is better than booze. They came back later, but I haven't gone back to drinking."

"So, how's your new life in Irkutsk?"

"Not great."

"Why?"

"Money. I keep having to shoot bears. I can get six thousand rubles for a skin, a month's salary! I've promised one to two or three people who've already paid me."

"In France we have a saying about people who sell a bearskin before . . ."

"I know, don't tell me. So do we."

"Really, not even one small vodka?"

"No, I *told* you, fucking hell."

APRIL 7

A whole hour cleaning the cabin. My reed broom works wonders. I sponge off the oilcloth and polish the windows with vodka. Because it's housekeeping day, I prepare my *banya*. In the evening, shiny as a ruble, I'm at the table with my glass of vodka, the kasha is cooking, the kettle's on, the candles are dripping, and the lake is creaking: everything's in its place doing its duty. The barometer is dropping like a stone; I can hear the tops of the cedars whistling.. . .

APRIL 8

Storm.

All that's left of my life are the notes. I'm keeping a diary to stave off forgetting, as a supplement to memory. Without a record of one's exploits, what's the point of living? The hours stream by, and each day vanishes into a triumph of nothingness. The private diary: a commando operation against the absurd.

I archive the passing hours. Keeping a journal makes life fruitful. The daily appointment with the blank page forces one to pay better attention to the doings of the day—to listen harder, to think more clearly, to see more intently. It would be grim to have nothing to inscribe in one's notebook in the evening. The daily composition is like having dinner with a fiancée: in order to know what to tell her later on, it's best to think about it during the day.

Outdoors, chaos. The wind is carving the snowdrifts with its teeth. Gusts are giving the edge of the forest a whipping. The cedars are in the front line, taking their punishment. Torn branches sail over the crowns of the trees, which the tempest seems bent on uprooting. A sad force, the wind, laboring in vain. Watching this fury with a good smoke, warm by the stove, is one definition of civilization.

In the evening, I slowly get drunk. The cabin: a cell of inebriation.

APRIL 9

Still storming. Inexhaustible, the wind, leading the assault against the skirt of the forest. Why this thirst for revenge? Its rage against what endures . . . The lake, perfectly polished, gleams, stripped of all snow. I go for a little walk on the ice, pushed along by the wind. A blast tears off my *shapka*, which whirls out of sight in ten seconds, carried off at sixty miles an hour. I'm almost two miles out on the lake. I rig up a turban from my scarf and pull my hood down tight. I hadn't anticipated having so much trouble getting back to the shore without crampons, going against the wind. I have to get down on my knees to offer less resistance. I progress by wedging my feet into the edges of cracks. Crawling across a frozen lake, bowed down before a storm, is a lesson in humility.

With a few more miles per hour, the wind would sweep me off to the middle of the lake like a hockey puck, forcing me to go ask for help on the other shore, fifty miles away in a village in Buryatia: "Hello, pardon me, the wind just blew me in."

*

Tonight the cabin creaked in every joint, adding the moans of the wood to the explosions of the ice. If I were superstitious, I'd be aghast at the noise.

Trapped, I'm angry. And calm down when I read this in Defoe's *Crusoe*: "The 24th (December). Rain all day all night, no stirring about for me."

APRIL 10

Dawn revealed a cold, blue day. The lake, washed. The world is new, burnished by forty-eight hours of fury. I drink my tea outside, at my table, in the refreshed atmosphere. Not a breath of wind. I detect a muffled humming, the tinnitus of solitude.

A visit to my wooden crates. My supplies are dwindling. I have enough pasta left for a month and Tabasco to drench it in. I have flour, tea, and oil. I'm low on coffee. As for vodka, I should make it to the end of April.

In the afternoon, I try out a new fishing spot an hour's tramp to the north, at the mouth of a little river, below a slope covered with sturdy conifers. The hole doesn't produce much: an hour to catch one char. I stay there until dusk, sitting on the stool, waiting for a twitch on the line. Fishing: the last clause in the pact signed with time. If you go home empty-handed, it means that time made the only catch of the day. I'm willing to spend hours sitting still. All that patience might bring me a fish. If not, too bad; I won't be angry at those hours for my disappointment. There aren't that many activities that risk being reduced to a vague hopefulness. Personally, I don't believe in Messiahs anymore, and will await the coming only of fish.

In the evening, after dealing with the sole char of the day, I finish *Crusoe* and begin *Justine; or, The Misfortunes of Virtue.* These two books should be read together. Not in order to imagine Justine arriving on a castaway's island, but because Robinson tries to re-create civilization and reinvent morality, whereas the Marquis de Sade tries to dynamite the former and soil the latter. Two servants of culture at opposite ends of the spectrum.

APRIL 11

After an overnight lull, the wind has doubled in strength. At two in the afternoon, it dies down again. The clouds open, soaking Baikal in sunshine. When a cloud counterattacks, the ice grows dull, and areas still bathed in light become striped with shadows. The gray knife blade gains ground, sliding over the ivory; the sun regroups, breaks through, and darkness ebbs away. The light is playing at games of wind and chance.

Amid all this mottling, four points stand out. My binoculars reveal some people on bicycles. For a moment I consider putting out the stove to keep the chimney from revealing my presence, but then I feel ashamed of that thought.

They have passed Middle Cedar Cape and have altered course. They're coming toward me. They'll be here in twenty minutes.

Sergei, Ivan, Svieta, and Igor work in the hydroelectric plant in Bratsk. During their winter vacation, they get on their bikes and ride along the frozen trails. I serve them tea; they unpack quantities of cold cuts and a huge jar of mayonnaise, which they carefully spread on every slice of sausage.

"Would you like more tea?" I ask.

"No," replies Igor, dipping a sausage in the mayonnaise. "We're going to have lunch in Elohin in about an hour."

"You've got a lot of titmice around here," remarks Svieta.

"Yes. They're my friends, and they're teaching me Russian."

They give me strange looks and eventually pack up to leave.

APRIL 12

I'm going to Elohin. I felt like having one of those *banyas* Volodya knows how to prepare, with the temperature at 200° F and beer to drink outside, our bodies steaming under the wooden awning as we look out at the mountains. En route, two hours north of my cape, I leave my sled at the mouth of a frozen river that slices through the forest with its icy blade. The crampons are gripping well, and I climb up from 2,600 feet through walls of schist bristling with denuded fir trees. The surface is only a bridge: I can hear water running beneath the vault. Red saplings grow along the edges, and their frozen debris streaks like blood through the crystal body of the ice. Winter is a vise.

From the lower river, it's still a little over seven miles to Elohin. Some wide faults force me to make many detours, seeking a way through the labyrinth of gaps and sometimes leaping over the fissures. Gusts of wind chivy along snaking lines of fine snow. I like walking on ice: in moonlight, it's one of the few places where you can be sure you won't be crushing little critters. The perfect terrain for those Jain priests who strive not to harm the tiniest gnat....

The veins in the ice. Like following the thread of a thought. If nature thinks, landscapes express the ideas. We ought to draw up a psychophysiology of ecosystems by attributing an emotion to each one. There would be the melancholy of forests, the joy of mountain torrents, the hesitation of bogs, the strict severity of peaks, the aristocratic frivolity of lapping waves. . . . A new discipline: the anthropocentrism of landscapes.

Volodya teases me when I show up at his door.

"You didn't bring any flowers for Irina?"

"Offering women flowers is a heresy. Flowers are obscene sex organs; they symbolize ephemerality and infidelity; they spread themselves wide open at the roadside, on offer to every passing breeze, the mouthparts of insects, clouds of seeds, and the teeth of animals. They're trampled, picked, and sniffed by noses. One should bring the woman one loves stones, fossils, some gneiss, I mean something that lasts forever and won't wither and fade."

That's what I would have liked to reply to Volodya, but my Russian is too weak, so I say, "Yes, I did have some, but they shriveled on the way. The *banya*, Volodya—it's ready?"

"It's waiting for you, pal."

That evening, I sit on the bench with Volodya's cat on my lap and watch Buryatia's lights go out. It's 10° F; the horizon is a sheet of satin. A snapping noise makes the cat's ears prick up; a dog barks.

Eleven o'clock. Volodya hasn't turned off the radio. I'm lying on the floor in the toasty cabin; we're listening to the main station. They announce the disaster. The Polish government's Tupolev jet has crashed near Smolensk. The Polish president and dozens of officials are dead. It seems there were no survivors. The plane was bringing a Polish delegation to a ceremony in honor of the victims of the Katyn Forest massacre, for which Moscow has finally agreed to admit responsibility.

"Volodya?"

"What?"

"This isn't the first time a Russian plane has wiped out some Poles.

"That's not funny, fuck that, not funny at all."

APRIL 13

Throughout the night, the radio spat out its news. In my half-sleep, I heard the growing toll: ninety-five dead...ninety-six dead...ninety-seven dead....At around two o'clock, I stopped up my ears with chewed paper. I tore out a page of *Lord Jim*, masticated it slowly (evil-tasting ink), and used Conrad's literature as earplugs, thinking I would hear the sea.

This morning, Volodya takes me along to inspect his trap line. The job of a forest ranger is to keep poachers from massacring the animals. Volodya carries out his mission strictly, and strictly within the boundaries of the preserve. His cabin sits on the southern bank of the Elohin River, the northern boundary of the nature preserve. On the other side, the taiga is no longer protected, and that's where Volodya sets his traps.

He's wearing his skis: horsehide strips tacked onto a pair of wooden runners. I'm wearing snowshoes. It takes three hours to check the traps. We sink deeply into the powder, working our way along the joint between the mountain slope and the wooded shelf at its base. The jays signal our approach. Volodya's young dog keeps raising false alarms, having not yet learned that one doesn't disturb the master over a squirrel. Volodya is training him with gobs of yelling: "These dogs don't know a thing, fucking hell!" Out of fifteen traps, two minks. Volodya swears that the forest is empty and that life was better in the old days. What the Americans did with the prairie bison, the Russians did with their mustelids: they've exterminated the weasel family to put people in furs. One day, man enters the woods, and the gods withdraw.

I will have learned that one can live near a gigantic skating rink, feed on caviar, bear paws, and moose liver, wear mink, stride through the woods with a rifle slung over one's shoulder, witness each morning, when dawn touches the ice, one of the loveliest sights on the planet, and still dream of life in an apartment equipped with the latest robotics and high-tech gadgetry. The eremitic temptation follows an immutable cycle: one must first suffer from indigestion in the heart of the modern city in order to dream of a cozy cabin in a clearing. Bogged down in the grease of conformity and padded in the fat of comfort, one becomes attuned to the call of the forest.

At noon I head for home. A dusting of snow covers the ice; slippery going for my boots. I'm eager for a solitary evening. Mist veils the slopes. The shore changes shape again and again.

APRIL 14

The winter just won't quit. Last night: 5° F. No sign of a thaw. Snowflakes fall from dawn to dusk, making a silky rustling. I spend the day in my mother cabin, my egg, my lair, crossing the threshold gratefully, feeling myself enveloped in that good warmth. The hours pass slowly through the window. I'm a bit bored. This day is a slightly leaky faucet from which every hour slowly drips. As a companion, boredom is passé, but one adjusts anyway, although time does start tasting a little like cod-liver oil. Then suddenly, that taste is gone and with it, all boredom: time has become once more that light-footed and invisible procession, making its way through Being.

APRIL 15

It takes me two and a half hours to get out of the forest. I'm heading up the second valley to the south of my cabin, looking for a bivouac. Despite my snowshoes, I sink in halfway up my thighs. Every step is a major battle. I reach the upper edge of the forest at seven in the evening, soaked. I choose a shelf at an altitude of 4,000 feet, above a scree slope. About 300 feet below me, I can make out the tracks of a wolverine. Wolverines don't hibernate, and this one has trekked across the flank of the mountain. The cold is brutal. Dwarf pines exposed by the wind crawl up among some rust-colored boulders. Buryatia is a red streak to the east. I cut armfuls of branches to make myself a mattress, and start a fire in the gathering darkness. I pitch the tent, toss in my mattress and sleeping bag. I cook some pasta over the fire, then lounge on my bed of branches, softer than a Byzantine sofa. My fire sits between two boulders about five feet high, and their sides reflect the heat. It's minus ten or twenty degrees Fahrenheit, but I'm warm in my band shell of rocks heated by the flames. And I stare at the precise spot where sparks from the fire, shooting into the sky, grow pale and glitter with a last brilliance before melting into the stars. It's hard to convince myself to go inside my tent; I'm like a kid who doesn't want to turn off the TV. From my sleeping bag, I can hear the wood crackling. Nothing is as good as solitude. The only thing I need to make me perfectly happy is someone to whom I could explain this.

APRIL 16

I open the zipper, blink in the raw sunshine, rejoice in the blue sky, sit up, and discover the image of the plain, gloriously empty at the bottom of its basin, 2,600 feet below. That's how today begins. Last night a lynx visited my camp, leaving tracks around my tent.

The euphoria of camping mornings! There you are, above the forest; you have survived the night and received a little lagniappe of life.

I climb 1,300 feet higher, straight up from the campsite. At ten in the morning, I'm only 1,640 feet from the summit ridge. The lakeshore traces a sine wave: the capes for crests, the bays for hollows. The black scallops of the wooded salients bite into the icy plain, undulating like a battle diagram of enemy lines falling back and charging forward. I return to my fire, rekindle it, make tea, break camp, and go home. The lynx checked out the wolverine's tracks before heading into the forest; the snow is crisscrossed by the tracks of minks, hares, and foxes. The forest thrums faintly with invisible life. Bushy lichens caress my face. I squint at the larches: they look like giants armed with bludgeons. If the desert hermits had retreated to the taigas, they would have invented religions peopled with joyous spirits and animal gods. The desert is desiccating, and I think about St. Bernard congratulating himself, after a walk, for having noticed nothing of the outside world.

I'm back in my cabin in three hours. It's 28° F, and I have lunch outdoors, at the lakeshore table. The titmice waltz, intoxicated with warmth. The first full-blown all-out day of spring is an important date in a man's year.

Shadows descend and, nibbling at the white plain, cross the lake to enshroud the Buryat mountains lounging on the opposite shore, convinced that sunset would pass them by.

APRIL 17

A hermit does not threaten human society, of which he is at most the living critique.

The vagabond steals and scrounges. The rebel-of-the-moment declaims on TV. The anarchist dreams of destroying the society in which he conceals himself. Today's hacker plots the collapse of virtual citadels in his bedroom. The anarchist tinkers with his bombs in saloons, while the hacker arms his programs at his computer, but both need the society they deplore and target for destruction—which is their raison d'être.

The hermit stays off to one side in polite refusal, like a guest who, with a gentle gesture, declines the proffered dish. If society disappeared, the hermit would go on living as a hermit. Those in revolt against society, however, would find themselves technically out of work. The hermit does not oppose, but espouses a way of life. He seeks not to denounce a lie, but to find a truth. He is physically inoffensive and is tolerated as if he belonged to an intermediate order, a caste halfway between barbarians and civilized people. The chivalrous hero of the twelfth-century epic poem Yvain, the Knight with the Lion, driven mad by the loss of his lady love, wanders naked in a forest until he is taken in and cared for by a hermit, who restores his reason and leads him back to civilization. The hermit: a passeur, a go-between of worlds.

At four in the afternoon, I close Chrétien de Troyes and set off to fish at hole number two, an hour's slog to the north.

(Hole number one is the spot out in front of the cabin.) The shore slips by, harsh and austere. There is joy in these woods but not an ounce of humor. Maybe that's what makes the faces of hermits so stern and Thoreau's writings so serious. I catch three char just under eight inches. They wind up on the stove, stuffed with blueberries, in a drizzle of oil. The flesh is tasty. Fresh, it goes well with vodka. Everything goes well with vodka. Except a woman's kisses. No danger of that.

APRIL 18

Sergei arrives at my cabin at eight in the morning. He's been visiting the Volodya up in Elohin, and I didn't hear his car out on the lake. As usual, he pops in without knocking—and I let out a yell, then take a long minute to recover my inner equilibrium, upended by the intrusion. My tea isn't even ready, so at least I didn't spill that.

"Your cabin, you keep it nice. With Volodya, it's what we call a *German* cabin."

"Oh, really?"

"You want to come to Pokoyniki? I'll bring you home again."

"Okay. . . . We'll have some tea, though?"

"No, just come, we're in a hurry."

Ten minutes later, I shut the padlock and climb into the car. We slip off to the south. In Russia, everything happens in a hurry: life is a drowsy thing shaken by spasms. In Pokoyniki, big doings. Sergei and Yura-with-the-pale-eyes have taken advantage of the frozen lake to build a pontoon on pilings—a platform baptized "the island"—out in the big marsh that prolongs the bay on its northern flank. With wooden levers, jacks, and ropes, we spend the afternoon hoisting a metal railroad car onto the wooden platform. Inside: a bed and a stove.

"The shoreline marks the boundary of the preserve, and the limit of its jurisdiction," announces Sergei. "So the island will be independent territory."

"Free?" I ask.

"Yes, free and independent. We have just created the *free and autonomous territory of Pokoyniki.*"

In the forest, shadows slip through the larches: horses are moving fluidly among the tree trunks. Their hooves crunch through the snow crust with the sound of a fist punching a feather pillow, and their nostrils give off plumes of vapor. These animals belonged to a herd maintained by the employees of the meteorological station at Solnechnaya, a little over a mile north of Pokoyniki, but they returned to the wild in 1991, when their caretakers abandoned the station at the collapse of the Soviet Union. At dusk, a four- or five-year-old horse comes wandering among the cabins, his head hanging. He has left the herd to die and lies down facing the lake. Sergei heaves a sigh, then dispatches him with a dagger thrust to the carotid. We chop him up with axes. Jays take their posts at the tops of the pines, and the entrails tumble out with a slurp, silky and perfectly coiled together, steaming in the cold. Night falls on this bloody affair. The dogs, who had been awaiting their turn, are given the go-ahead.

That evening, Pokoyniki is the scene of considerable excitement: the new director of the nature preserve, S.A., has come to visit his rangers, accompanied by his henchmen, who busily unload the vodka and cognac. I look longingly at those crates, because there's enough there to erase from my memory the sight of that horse panting hard as it gave up the ghost. Natasha has prepared some venison soup. A buffet in the Russian style is spread out on the table: a pell-mell of grilled catfish filets, a haunch of moose, and Siberian sausages. Everyone drinks into oblivion.

"Where were you born, Director?" I ask.

"In the Republic of Tuva."

"That's Lenin's native region," says Sergei.

"Well, then," I suggest, "let's drink to dictators who govern empires and nature preserves."

"And also to Tupolevs," adds one of S.A.'s thugs.

"Why?" I ask.

"The best plane in the world: the Poles just bit the dust in one."

Natasha offers the director a bag of frozen fish. Businessman though he may be, S.A. can't conceal the twinkle of delight in his eyes. Hereabouts people still haven't forgotten the hard times of the past.

APRIL 19

The cognac didn't agree with me. It's nine in the morning and I have a railroad tie stuck crosswise in my head. Yura with the fog-gray eyes awakens me: we have to go pull in the nets. Sasha of the missing fingers accompanies us. I nurse my hangover in the van, collapsed on some coils of rope, and listen to the two men rattle on about their favorite theme: "Why are there so many Muslims in your country?"

For a muzhik, France offers two subjects of astonishment: that the people of Napoléon's Grande Armée beg for government help when faced with not even an inch of snow, and that they let their cities burn while they have three thousand soldiers deployed in the mountains of Afghanistan. Sasha asks me about these things every single time we meet.

The ice-fishing shelter is nine miles from Pokoyniki. Inside the corrugated metal cabin, a wooden floor with a cut-out allows access to the fishing hole below. A gas stove heats the place, and we work in woolen shirts. We begin by raising many hundreds of feet of cordage with a hand winch that creaks at each turn. For two hours, Yura turns the handle, staring into space. The net surges up from the depths. The two Russians haul the nylon tresses from the water and harvest the omul, a freshwater whitefish endemic to Lake Baikal. The plastic tubs fill with hundreds of fish. In the eerie turquoise light, the lake offers its treasures. The strangest thing is that it keeps giving them to us on demand after thousands of years. Lunch: five fish tossed into a pot and sluiced with three glasses of *samogon*, the caramel-colored moonshine Sasha makes himself in his dacha at Severobaikalsk. Sergei drives me back home. We sit silently, gliding slowly over a surface worthy of an artist's brush: the marbling of the ice, the chaotic sculptures, the army of pines beneath their snowy burden, and the black granite draperies compose on the canvas of the sky a tortured tableau compared to which the desolate landscapes of the nineteenth-century German Romantic artist Caspar David Friedrich look like Haitian folk art.

We're stopped short by a crevasse.

"This one opened up today," Sergei announces.

"How will we get past?" I ask.

"A 'trampoline'. . ."

"And for your return trip?"

"A detour."

The two edges of a fracture are not always on the same level. As it shifts, the ice may raise one of the lips, and by using this discrepancy, drivers sometimes succeed in launching their vehicles over such obstacles. I have confidence in Sergei, but I feel a twinge when, going full blast from a head start of a good 160 feet, he crosses himself.

We make it.

APRIL 20

Here the journal breaks off for eight days for administrative reasons. The Russian authorities require my return to civilization to seek an extension of my visa. I tear myself away from the lake, take planes, besiege diplomatic and cultural officials who hibernate year-round more deeply than bears, obtain the stamp I covet, batten down my hatches so I won't get sucked into the big city, sleep five tense hours a night, get horribly drunk, heave another load of provisions and summer equipment into the back of a truck, retrace my steps, arrive at the lakeshore off the southern tip of Olkhon Island, and find the hydrofoil that had recently delivered me waiting for me there.

APRIL 28

Hydrofoils are the gem of Russian iron and steel metallurgy. Powered by a propeller, the machine moves on a cushion of air. So it couldn't care less about the fissures that scar the ice this late in April. Within four hours, we reach Pokoyniki, making as much noise as a massive Antonov airlifter. While I was gone, the lake surface has turned milky: melting slightly, the ice now has a nacreous crepe surface that crackles faintly underfoot. Passing the hamlet of Zavorotni, I stop in to visit V.E., who entrusts two of his twelve dogs to me. Aika is a black female; Bek, a white male. They are four months old. They will bark if bears begin approaching the cabin toward the end of May. I also have my distress flare gun. If attacked, you just fire at the animal's paws: the detonation and fireworks usually persuade the bear to buzz off.

I regain the cabin as happy as a foot soldier diving into his bunker. Depending on my mood, my shelter is an egg, a womb, a coffin, or a wooden ship. I bid farewell to my friends. Oh, the happiness that wells up as the rumbling of their engine dies away...

APRIL 29

Winter is still here. Only the pale face of the lake signals that spring is waiting in the wings.

Some snow has melted in the clearing, revealing the trash my predecessor accumulated over twenty years. Capable of superhuman efforts to repel an enemy, Russians can't summon the energy to throw garbage into a ditch. I cart tires, wrecked engines, and damaged motor parts off behind the *banya*. I restore the clearing to emptiness. A mist runs along the shores, snagging itself on the pines, sometimes dawdling enough to let a beam of sunshine slip through. Surrounded by fairyland, I go fishing. The dogs follow me everywhere. My shadow has become a dog. The two little creatures have placed themselves in my hands. A humanist animal, the dog believes in us. Wherever water seeps onto the ice, lapis-blue reflections bloom on the creamy glaze. The dogs wait patiently by the ice hole. I give them the guts of the three char I catch.

My round trip to the city has reinforced my love of cabin life. Cabins are the votive lights hung on the roof of the night.

APRIL 30

The taiga is black. The trees are shedding their snow. Dark patches appear on the mountains. Aika and Bek rush up outside the window at first light. When two little dogs celebrate your advent in the morning, night takes on a flavor of expectation. A dog's fidelity demands nothing, not a single duty. Canine love is satisfied with a bone. Dogs? We make them sleep outdoors, we speak roughly to them, snap at them, feed them on scraps, and now and then—*whap!*—a kick in the ribs. What we deal out to them in blows, they give back to us in drooling adoration. And suddenly I see why man has made the dog his best friend: this is a poor beast whose submission demands nothing in return, a creature corresponding perfectly, in other words, to what man is capable of giving.

We're playing on the lakeshore. Aika has found a deer bone, and I'm throwing it for them. They never tire of bringing it back to me; they'd keep going till they dropped dead. These masters teach me to inhabit the only country worth living in: the moment. Man's particular sin is to have lost this frenzy the dog has for retrieving the same bone. For us to be happy, we have to cram our homes with dozens of more and more sophisticated objects. Advertising urges us to "Go fetch!" The dog has admirably solved the problem of desire.

A long trek to South Cedar Cape with the little guys. The wind has come up and the sky is in shreds. Shafts of sunlight strafe the taiga through the clouds with tawny streaks and stamp it with yokes of gold; sometimes the light strikes a section of moldered cliff face, bathing it in brightness. Old ice faults can be treacherous where they haven't refrozen solid, because the eye cannot gauge the thickness of the surface. The dogs stop short, whimpering, before an area gorged with water, and I must advance carefully to show them they can follow. An eagle wheels high overhead. The wind kicks up sheaves of spangles, which turn into pyrite dust when they hit a sunbeam. The forest grumbles at the gusts. Spring has marshaled its forces here; I feel them, ready to attack, not yet daring to retake the territory.

The sky is insane, in a fluster of fresh air, dazed with light. Images of intense beauty spring up—and vanish. Is that the apparition of a god? I'm incapable of taking the slightest photo, which would be a double offense: a sin of inattention and an insult to the moment.

When we reach the cape where I wanted to test the fishing, a little over six miles from the cabin, I don't even have time to get out my ice drill. The enraged wind orders a retreat. I go home at a run, the dogs on my heels. We're waylaid by some fierce blasts, which suck up particles of abrasive crystal. The dogs protect their noses with their forepaws. For two hours, we fight our way toward the cabin against an invisible hand.

Tomorrow is May Day. Will the traditional lilies of the valley bloom on the taiga?

✸✸✸✸✸✸✸✸✸✸✸✸✸✸✸✸✸✸✸✸✸✸✸✸✸✸✸✸✸✸

The Animals

MAY 1

Last February, a good mile to the north of the cabin and within the orbit of a bay, Volodya T. set up a net to catch catfish. It lies out on the ice, attached to wooden stakes. I break open the old hole and thrust in the net, at the bottom of which I've hooked two char heads. The dogs stand guard in case any catfish come out of the hole to pounce on me.

I am the emperor of a mountainside, lord of my puppies, king of North Cedar Cape, protector of titmice, ally of lynxes, and brother of bears. I am above all a little tipsy because after two hours of cutting wood, I've just polished off the dregs of a bottle of vodka.

Living in a nature preserve is symbolic: man is just passing through. What trace of him is left? Footprints in the snow. Across the lake, on the Buryat shore, there is a *biosphere polygon* off-limits to all visitors. I find it poetic, this idea of turning stretches of the Earth into sanctuaries where life would go on without mankind. Animals and gods would flourish there, all unseen. We would know that life in its wild state was carrying on in that haven, and this thought would be an elixir. The point would not be to deny men the usufruct of the forests, barrens, and seas, but to protect a few selected acres from our appetites. The pretentious pedants of this world, however, are ever watchful, polishing up their speeches on the necessity of an ecology in the service of mankind. They would never allow seven billion human beings to be barred from the tiniest hankie-size sliver of the planet....

MAY 2

Hail is blurring the bronze of the taiga. The heavens have decided to send something besides snowflakes. A day for reading Mircea Eliade (a book for awaiting spring: *The Myth of the Eternal Return*) and for cleansing the clearing of the last of Volodya T.'s debris. Later in the day, I try out a new hole at the mouth of the North Cedar River. Now I have four fishing holes: in front of the cabin, at the tip of the cape, an hour's tramp to the north, and at the heart of the bay where I reactivated the catfish trap yesterday. Sitting on my stool, I smoke, keeping an eye on my fly line.

The dogs twine constantly around my legs; in me they have found someone who responds to their affection. They neither rely on nor delight in their memories. Between longing and regret, there is a spot called the present. Like jugglers who ply their trade while standing atop the neck of a bottle, we should train ourselves to balance in that sweet spot. The dogs manage it.

When he entrusted the puppies to me, V.E. from Zavorotni told me, "Don't let them get too close to you." I'm the most pathetic dog trainer east of the Urals, incapable of forbidding Aika and Bek from bubbling over with affection. People teach a dog how to lie down—and announce that they're *training* him. I accept the high jinks of the two little creatures and all it costs me is their paw prints on my pants legs.

We return home with dinner: three spotted char. Tonight the dogs will get the heads and entrails mixed into their mush of flour and lard. In the distance, the sun is cutting its way through the clouds here and there. This would have been a good spot for Paradise: infallible splendor, no serpents, impossible to live naked, and too many things to do to have any time left over for inventing a god.

MAY 3

This morning, dawn is tangled up in frilly tulle. I climb up toward the head of the "white valley." The dogs are struggling like dements to follow me, collapsing through the flat tracks of my snowshoes. At the heart of the combe, at the place where I turn up the flank to reach the granitic ridge, a bear has crossed through, heading for the other side of the valley. Hibernation is over. The awakening of the bears, the arrival of the wagtails, and the cracking of the ice are ambassadors of spring. I've got my flare gun at my waist, the dogs as scouts: I'm not at risk. The bears, on the other hand, know that man is a wolf to them, and they avoid encounters.

I'm at 3,280 feet, on the edge of the ridge. Sitting on a branch of dwarf pine, leaning back against a boulder, dangling my legs over the drop with a stand of golden larches far below, I watch the morning mist reach the lakeshore. Its billowy wave flows up against the lower edge of the forest. I love mist, that incense of the earth. I trim a Partagás. A lover of Havanas enjoys surrounding himself with smoke. Offerings in an inoffensive sacrifice, the puffs bind men to the gods. Every smoker dreams of disappearing into his own cloud.

MAY 4

The snows of yesteryear returned to the land today. A sidecar motorcycle appears on the northern horizon and stops at my shore. The dogs don't bark: not a good omen regarding their ability to warn me about approaching bears! It's Oleg, a fisherman I've met once or twice. He's traveling from Elohin to Zavorotni on an ageless Izh Planeta 750, a machine from the '80s that's better than the Ural 650 but lacks the chic of a military sidecar bike, as Oleg readily admits.

The vodka's good, snow is falling, and Oleg has brought cucumbers. We slice them thinly, and crunch one up with each glass. Oleg hasn't talked to anyone for a while.

"When I think that I was afraid of capitalists, but you, you're really nice. You have to come to Elohin more often. We're going to drive on the lake for another two weeks before it starts opening up everywhere and we can't take a step anymore without risking a pratfall. The ducks and geese will arrive, you'll see: one morning, there they'll be, back from China or Thailand or some other fucking paradise. Once some geese landed at my place, near the lake, and made a nest in my canoe. A few hunters showed up and wanted to blow their heads off. I told them, just try and I'll punch your faces flat. I don't like having birds asleep in my boat shot at. Last year, I found a baby seal beached on the pebble shore, and I fed it all summer long."

I imagine Oleg with his huge mitts feeding the little animal from a bottle. Earlier, when the bike was heading here, I thought, *Please let this bastard destroying my silence go on his way.* And here we are, two brothers polishing off a bottle.

"By the way," he says, "Irina sends you this little packet of yeast."

We've put paid to a liter of poison. Oleg takes off; I collapse on my bed.

MAY 5

Buryatia hands over the sun at six thirty a.m.

Yeast changes everything with blini.

The dogs have declared war on the wagtails.

A thin layer of snow makes the lake look like the world's largest salt flat.

It takes me three minutes to chop into firewood one of the pine log sections Sergei chainsawed three months ago.

It's 14° F at night and barely above freezing during the day.

Birch bark makes better tinder than dry moss.

The black dog stands out starkly on the ice. In the summer, she'll still be the one easiest to spot on the light gray lakeshore.

To sharpen the ax, a smooth stone patiently rubbed along the edge is enough.

The fish position themselves naturally at the very bottom of the fishing holes.

Vodka diluted with water makes a decent window cleaner.

It's stupid to hang the hurricane lantern from the cabin ceiling the way I did yesterday: the beams could have caught on fire.

There is pleasure in keeping one's home in order.

Cooking char en papillote without either scaling or gutting them intensifies the flavor of the fish.

At seven o'clock, the dawn light touches my table; at two in the afternoon, the foot of my bed. At six, the sun drops behind my peaks.

Not one insect has awakened yet.

It's at the fifth glass of vodka that resisting the next one becomes difficult.

Having little to do prompts one to pay attention to everything.

Those are the findings of today's inquiry.

MAY 6

Ice is the timekeeper. Spring will soon deliver the coup de grâce. Water has invaded the surface, carving it into countless vertical ruts, as if the ice were being eaten by worms. I must watch for the day when it breaks up into myriads of crystal bread sticks. The pitted surface no longer presents that lovely obsidian mirror, as sleek as metal. The mother-of-pearl crunches underfoot.

I take endless walks, flanked by Aika and Bek. I come and go, from one cape to another, and the crows cackle at each round trip.

MAY 7

There are six catfish caught in the trap, making this overcrowded net in the frigid water a nightmare. I understand why so many cultures consider this fish a demonic being. Catfish have maws like Chinese monsters and slimy yellow and greenish-bronze bodies. . . . They're somewhat like Tolkien's Gollum. I release four and keep the two biggest, which I kill with a blow just behind the skull. Even the dogs don't dare approach their flaccid bodies. Ah, the intense pleasure of giving a creature back its freedom! I mentally salute

Commander Charcot, a polar scientist who opened the cage door for his gull before sinking off the coast of Iceland in 1936. On the wooden table at the beach, I gut the fish, then stuff the stove with wood to cook it. The flesh of catfish is elastic, with a strong taste some find pleasant, others slightly nauseating. There are many ways of dealing with it, but the best is to dredge it in flour and crumbs so that the greasy fried coating masks the muddy flavor. (The English fry everything they get their hands on in bread crumbs, and I still recall the oily newspaper pages we had for napkins at a fish-and-chips place in Brighton.) I prepare a stew for the little dogs, saving a delicacy for myself: pan-fried catfish liver in a splash of vodka.

Months of devouring fish have produced a metamorphosis in me. My character has become lacustrine, more taciturn, slower, and my skin is whiter. I smell like scales, my pupils are dilated, my heart beats at a gentler pace.

A long walk on the lake to Middle Cedar Cape. The wind carries an odor of damp wood far and wide; temperatures slightly above freezing have released the perfume of the taiga. Spring is still only a frisson, but in the usual cold sky, the sun marks a hot spot. The water in the ice faults has melted. Whenever one of them is too wide, the dogs won't cross it. I take one in my arms, leap over the divide, then return for the other pup, who begs in faint whimpers not to be abandoned.

At Middle Cedar Cape, a ruined cabin. A man hid out there until the collapse of the Soviet Union, in 1991. When the KGB would come around, he'd flee into the mountains for a few days until the danger had passed. I couldn't find out whether he was a dissident or a deserter. Today there's only a hut with a caved-in roof. When I step inside it, I think about that guy. After Yeltsin came to power, the fellow returned to

Irkutsk and promptly died there. I would have liked to meet him; he would always have been welcome in my cabin. In the wreckage of the beams, I find a cup and the base of an oil lamp.

In Russia, the forest holds out its branches to the ship-wrecked. Yokels, nonentities, bandits, the pure of heart, rebels, those who can bear to observe only unwritten laws—they all head for the taiga. A forest has never refused anyone asylum. As for the princes, they used to send their woodcutters to chop down the trees. To govern a country, the rule is to clear the land. In an orderly realm, the forest is the last bastion of freedom to fall.

The State sees everything; in the woods, life is hidden. The State hears everything; the woods are a vault of silence. The State controls everything; here, only the immemorial codes apply. The State wants submissive subjects, pinched hearts in presentable bodies; the taiga loosens up souls and returns men to the wild. Russians know that the taiga is there if things go wrong; it's an idea anchored in their collective unconscious. Cities are temporary experiments, provisional experiences that the forests will one day reclaim. To the north, in the vastness of Yakutia (a territory larger than Argentina), this digestion has already begun. Out there, the taiga is retaking coal mining cities abandoned at perestroika. In a hundred years, there will be nothing left of these open-air prisons but ruins buried under foliage. A nation prospers through the substitution of populations: men replace trees. One day, history turns around, and the trees grow back.

Refuseniks of every country, take to the woods! Consolation awaits you there. The forest judges no one and imposes its rule. It stages its annual party at the end of May: life returns and the copses swell with an electric fever. In winter, you'll never feel alone: the cries of the crow family, the visits of titmice, and the tracks of lynx dispel all anguish. As for melancholy, simply consider this beautiful principle of regeneration: trees die, fall, and rot. And on the humus, which is the memory of the forest, other trees are born and begin their one or two centuries of reaching for the sky.

Bek, the little white dog, is bleeding. The ice has scraped his right front paw pads. I massage them with a mixture of catfish fat and oil. Has evolution foreseen the eventual use of silurid liver for the healing of small Siberian dogs?

MAY 8

Across the gray and white plain fractured by its live-water wounds, I'm off to Elohin for a courtesy visit to Volodya. Bek's paw pads are better. The dogs trot along side by side, and we cover the distance in five hours. We had to find a way through the labyrinth of fissures in the middle of Elohin Bay; a big eagle was soaring overhead, keeping tabs, perhaps, on a dead seal.

I'm sitting at Volodya's table looking out the window at eternal Russia passing in a series of images. Russians use the word *glubiná*—depth—to refer to these far-flung zones, the deep country of the nation. Irina, her kerchief on her head, is feeding her goose in the vegetable garden. A billy goat goes by, followed by a cat. This window, which could be entitled *A Day in Siberia*, is like a painting by Ilya Repin, a Ukrainian whose realistic depictions of life at all levels of the social order became archetypes of the "Russian national style." Now the dogs are fighting. When they arrived in Elohin, Bek and Aika, all of four months old, rushed at Volodya's five mastiffs to have their hides. They took a drubbing, but I congratulated them on their fighting spirit. Volodya is holding a cup of tea in his huge mitt and eating a lemon as if it were an apple. On the radio, Yves Montand is singing *Autumn Leaves*, which crackles a bit. An announcer launches into a tribute to the glory of the Red Army. Tomorrow is May 9, Victory Day. It's 2010, and the Russians are still amazed at having beaten fascism. Sixty-five years are as nothing: they speak of the victory as if it were yesterday.

"Volodya, what's the news, aside from the fact that you won sixty-five years ago?"

"Nothing. Wait, yes, in Florida there's a black tide: all the American coasts are gummed up."

A tour of the stag traps. A simple procedure: a piece of sheet metal with five cuts sawn into it to form a central star is placed over a hole and covered with grass. A block of salt attracts the animal. When it steps onto the trap, it's snagged. Stag trophies go for a pretty price in the city. Man has felt himself duty bound to empty the forest.

That evening: "Chess, Volodya?"

"Yes. The second most intelligent game after tug-of-war."

We play, I lose, and finish Morand's biography of Fouquet, the fabulously wealthy superintendant of finances whom an envious Sun King finally sent to prison for life. I like to immerse myself in reading that transports me to the precise antipodes of my actual life. Exoticism: while the wind rustles gently through the Siberian cedars, I navigate through the political intrigues and dirty tricks of the court at Versailles, the animosities of Louis's chief minister, Mazarin, and the battles within the Roman Catholic hierarchy in France over the theological movement of Jansenism. Question: who would have lasted longer, Volodya at the court of Versailles, or the king's great general, le Grand Condé, out on the taiga? "Before Fouquet, nature itself trembles," writes Morand, evoking the monumental construction of the Château de Vaux-le-Vicomte, the first example of *le style Louis XIV*. "It is as if nature were razing herself to the ground, seeking to be forgotten, so often have the tragedians and preachers informed her that she has no rightful claims over mankind." It was to forget the warbling of tragedians and preachers that I installed myself in a cabin.

MAY 9

Morand, chapter 2: "There are three ways to begin one's life. With pleasure at first, and serious things later, or by working hard at the beginning so as to ease up toward the end, or by managing to pursue both pleasure and labor at once." The cabin follows that last prescription.

At eight in the morning, a bear of well over six hundred pounds comes prowling around the sandy embankment to the south of the small clearing at Elohin. Volodya has filled some cans with seal fat to attract the animals, and now he murmurs, "Ah, too bad it isn't about a third of a mile to the north, outside the preserve, we could shoot it." I feel suddenly numb with despair. We ought to have a little bit of our neocortex removed at birth to neutralize our desire to destroy the world. Man is a capricious child who believes the Earth is his bedroom, the animals his toys, the trees his baby rattles.

Yesterday's lesson has borne fruit. Aika and Bek stay close to me and away from the other dogs. When we return to the enclosure around the *izba*, my two little darlings are set upon by Volodya's howling pack. I plunge into the mêlée, kicking furry flanks right and left to protect my puppies while Volodya yells at me over the barking to "let them follow their fucking rules!" That's when the black cat that palled around with Aika the night before comes flying to the rescue and with a few swipes of his claws, routs the ringleaders. I immediately bestow upon him "the Imperial Order of the Northern Cedars for service rendered to my personal guard," and I head home after kissing Irina on her rosy cheeks and getting my chest crushed in Volodya's parting hug.

On the way back, a seal. He's sunning himself near a handy emergency escape fissure. I crawl over the ice, concealed by a ridge of ice chunks. Did he hear me? Was it Aika's black stain on the ivory tablecloth? I'm some two hundred yards away when he vanishes.

The weather has warmed up, and the chimney plume from my stove traces persistent spirals in the air, as reassuring as the evening cloud of cigarette smoke.

MAY 10

This morning, dawn has kept its promise again: the sun appeared, punctually, and the sky became a ceiling for an operetta theater. I go out onto the lake to get a good look at the mountain cleared of its snow. Only the summits and the depths of canyons are still white. On the lake, I leap over a fault—and its far edge snaps off: I've jumped too short and fall into the water, where the main thing is not to slip under the ice. I have a chilly walk back. The faults in the lake, like the crevasses of glaciers, greet overconfidence with the kiss of death.

In the afternoon, I go up to the waterfall. The snow in the understory still sticks to the snowshoes, and the dwarf pines hamper me more than ever. To make any headway, I have to use the scree slopes. As for the dogs, they're mastering the art of frisking among the rocks. At the edge of the cut leading to the waterfall, spring is preparing its rite. Fragile forces are erupting; velvety mountain anemones quiver in the sunshine; grasses are growing among the patches of crystalline snow. An expanse of white still shows my footprints, which a bear has followed before turning back to the river below. Ants flow up and down their towering cities of ice needles; it's as if they were observing some solar cult around a (slightly eroded) pre-Columbian temple. The torrent has broken free and dives beneath the ice down at the mouth of the valley. The mountain is melting. Its flanks are striped with living streams hurrying with girlish haste to plunge into the lake. Alder buds have popped out of their sheaths. Clumps of azaleas are sprinkled with violet flowers. Glossy leaves smell like beeswax polish. Nature's timidity is a prelude to its triumph.

Two opposing impulses foster this rebirth: the emergence of what was buried beneath the soil, and the overflowing of what was stored up in the heights.

What overflows: the water tumbling from the peaks, the freshets washing the faces of the slopes, the ants boiling out of their cauldrons, the sap pearling on the pine bark, the stalactites stretching for the earth, the bears and deer quitting the plateaus to scrounge for a pittance on the shores.

What emerges: the larvae in the ground that break out by the billions, the shoots, the flowers blooming on their stems, the schools of fish returning to the surface after their benthic winter. And I, tonight, will be tranquilly smoking in my cabin, right at the junction between this uprush and downpour.

Way up there, the waterfall is still frozen, but its liberation draws nigh. A matter of days.

I catch three char in one hour this evening. It's puzzling, but the lake never delivers more than that to me, as if it were adjusting my catch to my needs. There's a mystery there that acts as a caution against fishing fever. One day, a caveman must have fished for more than he could eat, announcing the advent of human hubris and our current pillaging of the planet. The other explanation for my meager results—and the more likely one—is that I'm a lousy fisherman.

Today I saw a seagull. And a female black grouse at the tip of North Cedar Cape. My eye fell on her by chance, otherwise I'd have passed blithely by, only inches away.

The evening arranges pastel reflections of blue and rose on the Buryat peaks. The mountains? Good enough to eat.

The ice won't last much longer. Near my watering spot, I open a breach a yard wide in half an hour, as if I were hacking through loaf sugar. In my new swimming hole, in the glow of hurricane lanterns, I immerse myself in the water. The Russians do this for the salvation of their souls in January, at Epiphany. At 36 or 37° F, water bites into your legs and winds up gripping your whole body. My cigar brings an illusion of warmth. The heart seems surprised at being subjected to such treatment. The human brain is a kind of aristocratic headquarters that enjoys commanding the body to do the labor of convicts. The gray matter bathes pleasantly in spinal fluid while the carcass breaks its back working.

I scramble out of the hole after I suddenly have a vision of enormous catfish teeming in the waters, along with some of Baikal's indigenous *Epischura* copepods seeking something to munch on. The lake is clean thanks to its scavengers.

MAY 11

I don't miss a thing from my former life. I'm struck by this certainty while spreading honey on some blini. Not one thing. Nothing, nobody. It's a worrisome thought. Can a man so easily shed the clothing fitted to his thirty-eight years of life?[11] When you organize your life around the idea of possessing nothing—then you have everything you need.

With my binoculars I spot a seal a good mile away. Drawing closer in an elaborate detour, I'm careful to keep the light behind me. Ice slabs from a breach in the ice about five yards across make a kind of floating bridge, and I keep my balance leaping from one to another. I've approached to within about a hundred yards of the seal when it vanishes, swallowed down by its hole in a brisk gulp.

This evening the little dogs spend two hours running after a wagtail that shows remarkable patience. After which, they squabble over a roe deer's hoof.

MAY 12

A day at North Cedar Cape:

Look at the sky at six in the morning. Light the fire (murmuring a few nice words to it), and go out to draw water. Note that the thermometer says 28° F. Pour boiling tea on a blini and eat it. Look outside again—but through the smoke of the first cigarillo. Finish *Promise at Dawn* while eating some blueberries from Irina. Visit the four anthills that surround my cabin, all spaced about three hundred yards apart, and check out the consolidation work under way. Use binoculars to search for the black dots of seals basking in the sun. Draw the oil lamp, trying to depict the transparency of the glass. Repair the knife sheath damaged during yesterday's outing. Chop wood. Feed the dogs some catfish mush. Cook the evening's kasha. Spend forty minutes at the nearest fishing hole catching the two fish that will accompany the kasha. Think about what this day might have been if my dear one, the only person on this earth whom I miss even when she's with me, had deigned to be here. Do not think about the reasons that led her not to come along. Get quietly drunk because of the impossibility of not thinking about the above. Rejoice at the coming of night that will hide the shit on my shitfaced face.

MAY 13

It's raining and it's cold and the cedar branches gleam and drip. Beauty will never save the world; it merely provides lovely settings in which men kill one another.

A gray silence has settled on the lake. What is this soft day brooding over? A last gasp from winter? No, spring is too far advanced. What's lovely about the seasons is that each one politely hands over its charge. Not one of them lingers too long. Finally, at around five o'clock, something happens: the clouds part. Blue sky dissolves the cotton wool. The gray mass is breaking up and scarves of mist drape themselves around the taiga's throat. Quick, a glass! May the vodka help me to better see the subtlety of these transformations! Oh, if I had some wine, . . . Well, the Kedrovaya will do, after all. At the fifth shot, I understand what's going on *inside* the clouds.

MAY 14

Time time time time time time time time time.

 Hmm?

 It passed!

MAY 15

The best way to kill the intensity of a moment is to feel obliged to catch it in a photo. I sit for an hour at the window while dawn churns out moments by the ton.

 The cabin is the railroad car in which I signed my armistice with time: I have made my peace with it. Letting it pass is simply common courtesy. From one window to the other, one glass to another, within the pages of a book, beneath closed eyelids, the main thing is to move aside to let it go on its way.

The gray wagtails are making their nest at the northeastern corner of the roof. The dogs have given up trying to get them. Sitting at my table, I watch the ice die. The blanket of snow is in tatters. Water has seeped in everywhere, mottling the surface with black blotches. The lake is suffering, unaware that men sit at its bedside. I am one of many keeping vigil.

 The day is marked by notes that measure out a solfeggio. The titmouse arrives at eight, the sunbeam hits the oilcloth at nine thirty, the seals appear in the middle of the afternoon, the little dogs gambol about at twilight, the moon's reflection blooms in the pail nightly: a perfect mechanism. These insignificant rendezvous are the immense events of life in the woods. I wait for them, hopefully. When they arrive, I recognize them, salute them. They prove to me that the poem respects its meter. The ancient Greeks watched for similar changes in the atmosphere: suddenly something was going on; the god was appearing. This feeling of startlement before a ray of light: wisdom or senility? Happiness becomes this simple thing: waiting for something you know will happen. Time turns into the marvelous organizer of these appearances. In cities the opposite principle is at work: there we require a permanent efflorescence of fresh surprises. The fireworks of novelty constantly interrupt the flow of hours and illuminate the night with their fleeting bouquets. In a cabin, one lives to the rhythm of the metronome rather than the glitter of pyrotechnics.

The dogs content themselves with endless repetitions. As soon as the event begins to take shape, they drool with impatience. If the unexpected occurs, if a visitor arrives, they growl, bark, attack. The enemy? Novelty.

Sometimes revelations rise from the depths of our own being. Instead of quivering before the signals of the world, we sense an inner impulse, the birth of an idea, an overwhelming desire. Then we feel like a world in ourselves, where gods and demons are locked in battle.

It rains again this afternoon. The clouds blow in from the west and stagnate over the basin of the lake. Off on the Russian plain, the reserves of humidity are apparently inexhaustible. Cawing crows skim the surface of the water, raindrops hammer the shingles, and the taiga seems like an army biding its time. Nature is going through a depressive phase.

In my case, stuck here alive in my wooden coffin, the dreaded hours arrive with the evening. Ghosts and regrets take advantage of the twilight to slip into my heart, launching their operations just when the light fails, at seven o'clock. I need vodka to repel them. Inventory of supplies: I have twenty-two liters of Kedrovaya, three liters of pepper vodka, twelve Partagáses, and five cartons of cigarillos (twenty to a box). Enough to fight the demons for a few months.

The courageous course would be to face things: my life, my times, and other people. Nostalgia, melancholy, reverie—these give romantic souls the illusion of a virtuous escape route. They pass for esthetic ways to stave off ugliness but are merely the *cache-sexe* of cowardice. What am I? Contemptible, frightened by the world, a recluse in a cabin off in the woods. A coward who silently soaks himself in alcohol to avoid witnessing the spectacle of his times or encountering his own conscience pacing up and down along the lakeshore.

MAY 16

Finally, the sky clears. I act like a Russian: for three or four days I've been waiting lethargically at the window, and with a bound, I rush outside, the dogs at my heels and three days' worth of provisions in my backpack. That's how the Russians cope: long days of inertia interspersed with periods of bustling activity. The ice is still holding up. I cut toward Middle Cedar Cape, intending to head up the valley that debouches there. I leap over the fissures, leaving ever greater margins of safety because the edges are getting thinner. I take refuge from a sudden downpour in the primeval forest that for millions of years has covered the alluvial plain of the river on which I've set my sights. My steps sink into the mosses. Ribbons of lichen loop like felt beneath the trees. The forest resembles the marshes of Walter Scott and the exotic undergrowth of *The Lost World*. The sun comes out to shoot its rays through the swirling fog. Birches line up in ivory aisles. The hardy *Rhododendron dauricum* gives off the smell of a very clean old lady, which stands out against the earthy odors of stumps clawed open by bears. The forest is full of its own breath. Confused by the profusion of scents, the dogs are beside themselves: Pandora's box has been opened a crack, and these treasures have seeped out. The Siberian taiga is a cold jungle. The queen of the elves could appear with all her court, parting the curtains of lichen with her hand, and I wouldn't be at all surprised.

Behind a string of willows in a strangely straight line, I discover a ditch colonized by shrubs. Twenty years ago, a trail linked the camp of some geologists to the lake, and the base mentioned on the map is still here, at 2,300 feet: four derelict *izbas* and two rusted sheet-metal trailers sit among the saplings. To the north opens a double valley where the thalwegs—the line defining the lowest points along the length of a valley or river bed—are separated by a ridge of stone. I struggle on a scree slope cluttered with dwarf pines, whose branches, lying like a net across the stones, present a supple, impassible wall. I retreat down into the combe, put on my snowshoes, and climb to the base of the rocky ridge. At around 3,300 feet, a shelf seems suitable for a bivouac. A storm breaks out, dumping all the water in the sky on our terrace of schist and granite. I hide the ice ax and crampons a hundred yards below us. The lightning terrifies Aika and Bek, who huddle under a birch tree. I admire them, these little creatures who set off for the mountain happy to be alive, without provisions or plans to return.

I cut strips of dwarf pine to serve as flooring for the terrace, then spend three solid hours trying to light a fire with waterlogged wood. A few pages of *Rameau's Nephew* finally catch. (Not the first time that Diderot has set something on fire.) An anemic flame rises from a tiny pile of shredded bark, dried against my skin. Fire, a poor animal wounded by the storm; I make it grow twig by twig. The flame wavers... and I feel as if I were dealing with a cardiac arrest. The flame grows: victory. I blow on it until I'm dizzy and obtain live coals. The dogs come to warm themselves in the flickering glow. Just when I'm setting up the tent, a fresh cloudburst: I retreat beneath my poorly stretched canvas as hail sparkles into thousands of diamonds during the nanoseconds of lightning. The tent bends, doesn't collapse, gets drenched. While the tempest bedevils the mountain and my panel of nylon, I learn that Diderot liked to relax every evening in the mellow light of the Palais-Royal. The wind dies down, the storm passes, the stars come back out and, oh joy, the embers are still alive. I stoke the fire and lie down with an anti-bear flare wedged close to my head in case we have visitors. Aika and Bek are curled around each other in the Siberian night like the symbol of yin and yang.

MAY 17

The sun is already high in the sky. The little dogs welcome my awakening. They must be expecting some snack, but I've nothing except a bit of bread. It would be best if they returned to the cabin, but they won't do that, and remain close to me. Dogs take us for their god and their mother, i.e., their master. I break camp and climb along the ridge for five hours. The dogs whine when they're stopped by a ledge; Aika then finds a way around and guides her clumsier brother. The ridge line straightens out and at 5,250 feet, I reach the layer of hardpack. Perched on a boulder, Aika and Bek contemplate the lake.

At the summit, elevation 6,890 feet, it's gulag cold. To the east, the heart of the nature preserve is revealed. The mountain chain running along Baikal collapses as soon as it crosses to the other side of the ridge. The view to the north grows narrow, running parallel to the shore. Baikal: a cameo set into a shrine. To the east, foothills roll out forests of gray pine, spotted with lakes and streaked with tributaries. The climate out on the taigas is harsher than that of Baikal. Asian timber companies drool over these virgin territories; the Chinese would love to get their hands on such reserves of wood and water, which would be like a second Manchuria for them, since they've exhausted the first one. Never in our history has a mass of humanity left a nearby depopulated area rich in resources unexploited for long. History is governed by the laws of hydraulics, and if we set China and Siberia up as hypothetical communicating vessels, Mongolia would be the connecting valve. If there were ever a struggle for control of the taigas here, my summit would make a good surveillance post. The Chinese will have the advantage of numbers and hunger; the Russians will have backwoods inaccessibility and their hatred of any threat to *mat rodina*, the motherland. The little dogs, noses tucked into their fur, are fast asleep.

We go back down through the northernmost canyon. At the halfway point, the walls draw together and a sudden forty-five degree dip in the slope forces me to cut steps in the snow. The dogs whimper, unable to advance. Then Aika launches herself onto the slide, counting on me to stop her, which I do, and Bek as well. The technique Aika has devised works well, and we reach the foot of the wall. Toward the bottom of the valley, I rejoin my tracks from yesterday, which have been crossed—and recently—by a bear: the prints are deep and the animal seems not to have shown the slightest interest in my trail. At the edge of the wood, the tongue of snow over the torrent has broken open, spitting out its flood of clear water. I make a fire to dry my clothes and nap in the wonderful sunshine.

Return to the lake via the geologists' trail. The sun and clouds are playing chess: they place their pieces on the marble board, where the white and black spots move around with the speed of cavalry charges.

MAY 18

At noon, I leave the cabin to ascend the "white valley," that curving combe of larches that cuts through the mountain a good half a mile to the north. Atop the rocky crest from which flow draperies of scree, the ravages of spring are clear: the lake is a mess.

To reach the summit that looms above the cabin, one need simply follow the serrate ridge. Beneath a Mediterranean sun, I pass turrets and rock pinnacles of Hercynian granite, rotten to the core. Small boulders not anchored to the slope by dwarf pines now roll beneath my feet and I'm afraid of crushing the dogs. By nightfall, after a third of a mile of tapering ridgeline larded with snow-filled couloirs, those steep, narrow gullies and fissures, I reach the summit, at 6,560 feet. Before me lies the arcature of the Baikal Range, crowned sixty miles to the north by Mount Chersky. Sharp rocky crests spread out like starfish in all directions. Areas where the snow has melted are covered with the lichens so prized by the deer. A few days ago, a bear passed through the small, narrow saddle not far below. Hegel's *So ist*—It is so—is the wisest thing to say before the incommensurable. I like the idea of having climbed up to find out what's on the other side of my domain. Baikal is a closed basin, containing its own species, governed by its own climate. The inhabitants live on its edges as if around a village square. Most of them have never come here to take a look behind the ramparts of the fortress. One can be content with never going outside. Or one can decide to go have a look.

In 1643 a band of Cossacks led by Kurbat Ivanov, the first Russian explorer to reach Baikal, arrived from the west and climbed these peaks one day bearing guns and daggers. They perched on the ridge and discovered in one fell swoop, four or five hours' march away, the Baikal Sea of which the various peoples of the taiga must have been telling them ever since the Yenisei, the mightiest river of Siberia. . . .

Crossing slippery slopes and unstable couloirs, I find a good shelf planted with dwarf pines at 5,250 feet, where I spend a divine night with the dogs, the lake, the peaks, and the starry fire-sparks that would like to join their sisters up in the heavens.

MAY 19

A rapid return: we slide through the couloirs to the first trees of the "white valley." A powerful wind blows from the north, exciting the dogs. A storm is brewing. I'm in the hammock with a cigar and Giono's *Song of the World* when it hits: in a few seconds the tempest sweeps down from the mountains and the wind begins chewing up the icy plain. Within ten minutes, the debacle ruins winter's attempt to keep order in the world. The spectacle of this season must have dismayed the Prussian generals; it's a Russian who celebrated the rite of spring.

The ice is breaking up: the water regains its freedom, cutting channels among the floes or submerging sections of the plain. The rain can't find its way to the earth. Whorls of water return to the sky in little whirlwinds. In the confusion, the cedars send signals of alarm. Aika and Bek have taken refuge beneath the stoop of the shed. The anthracite breaches of open water show up starkly against the routed pack ice. Wind flurries roil the waters. A rainbow, born at the tip of the cape, touches down in the middle of the lake, framing beneath its curve ebony clouds massed in the north. Lightning bolts strike just as the sky closes down, leaving only one shaft of light to turn the Buryat peaks blood-red as their range bears up under a ceiling of ink. I have just watched, in the space of ten minutes, the death of winter.

The storm carries its devastation off to the south. The lake settles down. In the cool air, beneath a satiny sky, the unleashed wind shoves the drifting ice around, and shards of the former stained-glass window break off at the slightest touch with a rustle like rough silk. The debacle has released the ebb and flow of the lake. I set my stool on a sheet of ice and spend the evening gently drifting. The water is back! The water is back! Nothing will be the same.

MAY 20

On this first morning of the lake's liberation, the wagtails indulge in feats of illusionism: they hop about on the invisible scales of ice a millimeter thick that cover the stretches of open water. Toward noon, a hard rain falls with a voluptuous rattling on the humus. The Earth is drinking its fill. The rivers run almost all the way to the lake; only a hem of ice masks their arrival at the shore. In years and centuries to come, these waters that quench my thirst will be churned by the swells of the polar sea. When you consider the voyage of a snowflake, from the peaks to the lake and the lake to the sea via the rivers, you feel like a poor excuse for a traveler.

I remove two bloodsucking ticks from Aika. Life is a business of exacting tribute, and it's the plants that pay for everyone else in the end!

MAY 21

The rafts of ice will shift about for a month at the mercy of the winds and currents, coming and going, and it's possible that one day my bay will be reclosed by pack ice. This morning the lake is a liquid plain. Not one ice cube on the oily black surface. I leave with the dogs for the Lednaya River, halfway between my cabin and Elohin, to try fishing there.

Along the shore, recent events have fostered an explosion of life. The day is full of flies. I nap on some sun-warmed rocks. On the embankments, clumps of anemones dot the sand. Ducks have landed in the open areas, eager for love and fresh water. They were living it up down south. They lift off clumsily when the dogs dash over to them. First men imitated birds to build planes, and now the first planes they built are imitated by ducks. The shoreline is in a permanent aerial ferment: eagles soar, geese patrol in gangs, gulls do nose dives, and butterflies, amazed at being alive, stagger through the air. Forty-eight hours have been enough for spring to bring off its putsch.

In the forest, the path traced by deer and bear tracks has opened up along the shore, a few yards behind the edge of the wood. Suddenly the doggies are barking: higher up on a rocky talus, a bear pokes its head through the rhododendrons. I hold Aika back by the scruff, while her brother cowers between my legs. Courage was doled out unevenly in that litter. Russians are emphatic on this point: when a bear shows up, do not run, do not look at the animal, don't make any sudden moves; just tiptoe off murmuring reassuring things. The problem lies in inspiration: what does one say to a bear? I'm unprepared and, retreating delicately, find nothing better than "Beat it, you big bunny!" It works: the animal forages its way off through the undergrowth.

I catch two char at the mouth of the river. We go home via the shore. I walk along with the distress flares glued to my hands. The beaches and bands of littoral ice are covered with bear tracks. I'm not afraid; I know they will not attack me. In case of anxiety, think only of the last pages of *Robinson Crusoe*, where Defoe describes the taciturn indifference of these beasts: "The bear was walking softly on, and offered to meddle with nobody...."

I reach the cabin, repair my fishing fly, feed the dogs, prepare my two fish, flick my knife into the wall, and go to bed with *The Song of the World*. Giono displays the usual reversal of values favored by all who convert to natural laws: he personifies things and naturalizes people. In his works, rivers have legs and the woodsmen have "bodies like rocks."

MAY 22

The wind is busy cuffing a stretch of open water a third of a mile long that runs beside the shore. Beyond it, a chum of floating ice is driven by the west wind, and frozen sheets are snapping apart like loaf sugar soaked with champagne. The lake gives off a scent of sex.

Diggers, borers, crunchers, kneaders and burrowers, scratchers, those with claws, and drills, and beaks or proboscises, the crawlers, walkers, fliers, and those who perch on the back of a stronger creature, and the imitators, the disguisers, those of the night, the day, and the twilight, those who see, those who smell: all are emerging from their torpor and coming to see the liberation of the waters the way friends welcome a prisoner the day he's released from jail. Despite their long sleep, these creatures have not forgotten their roles and reflexes. The insect hordes are poised to invade the woods, and I feel less alone.

In a cabin, life takes on a counterrevolutionary tone. Never destroy, the hermit tells himself, in reactionary mode, but conserve and carry on. The recluse seeks peace, unity, renewal, and believes in the eternal return. Why break with anything, for everything will pass—and come around again? Does the cabin have a political meaning? Living here adds nothing to the community of men; the hermitage experience adds nothing to the collective study of how to get people to live together. Ideologies, like dogs, remain just outside the hermit's door. Off in the woods—neither Marx nor Jesus, neither order nor anarchy, neither equality nor injustice. How could the hermit, preoccupied solely with the immediate, possibly care about foreseeing the future?

The cabin is not a base camp for reconquest but a hide-out, a port of call.

A haven of renunciation, not a headquarters for fomenting revolution.

An exit door, not a point of departure.

A wardroom where the captain goes to drink a last glass of rum before the shipwreck.

The hole where the animal licks its wounds, not the burrow where it sharpens its claws.

MAY 23

Last night, at three o'clock, barking sent me rushing from the cabin, flare gun in hand. A bear was wandering on the beach. At dawn, its tracks on the gray sand.

The open water continues to bring off victories. This morning it extends for over six miles between the drift ice and my shore, and the wind is pushing the ice raft farther out. The sun sparkles on the slush, while the beach remains in shadow. There's no sight more joyful: the first sunbeams enter the cabin to dance around the floor. The sun fusses over me like the dogs. During the day, the eye gleans all these images that dreams will cook up later on.

According to Kierkegaard in his *Sickness unto Death*, man knows three ages: those of esthetic and Don Juan–esque pleasure, Faustian doubt, and despair. To them must be added the age of withdrawal to the woods, as a sound conclusion drawn from the three earlier periods.

Around my neck I wear a small Orthodox cross, which shines in the sun when I chop wood with my shirt off. In my childhood I dreamed of a "Robinson Hood" with a blond beard who always wore on his breast the cross of Christ. I love that man who forgave adulterous women, strode along with his mouth full of pessimistic parables, denounced the bourgeois, and went off to kill himself atop a hill where he knew death was waiting for him. I feel I am a part of Christendom, those places where men—deciding to worship a god who preached love—allowed freedom, justice, and reason to invade their cities. What holds me back, however, is Christianity, the name given to that tinkering with the Gospel by the clergy, that alchemy by sorcerers in tiaras ringing little bells that has transformed a burning message into a penal code. Christ should have been a Greek god.

MAY 24

Last night I dreamed of a bear attack. They were jumping on the cabin roof, as agile as cats and as svelte as Afghan hounds. Pretty damn horrible. I suspect the newly pervasive smell of algae in the atmosphere of influencing my dreams and nudging them into Gothic territories.

A squadron of tufted ducks alights on a sheet of open water edged by three enormous festoons of ice, then takes off in perfect formation in the direction of Mongolia. A pair of mergansers likes it here in my bay. I spend hours peering through my binoculars studying their punkish crests. Some diving harlequin ducks come in for a full-tilt landing on a narrow canal. These ducks are dressed to kill, and when they fly off you just *know* they know where they're going.

At eight every evening, the sunlight manages to slip into a notch in the peaks to the south and shoot a long stream of russet gold onto the velvety foliage of the thorn bushes. I'm not interested in knowing whether God or chance is responsible for such beauty. Must you know the cause to enjoy the effect?

In the evening, I dine outdoors, before a bonfire out on the beach. Then I stay to watch the flames with the dogs, my hands warm in their fur, until the moon over the mountain gives the signal to go to bed.

MAY 25

I spend hours smoking in my hammock at the top of the hill, with the dogs in faithful attendance. In Paris, my loved ones think I'm wrestling with the Siberian cold, panting at my chopping block to cut wood in a blizzard.

The lake: a blue-leaded window with alabaster panes. Scales of ice glide toward the south. Lying out in the mild air, I watch these watery flocks on the move. Between the scales, the color of the water changes from hour to hour. Two sheldrakes zip over this leprous display so fast that I wonder if something is hot on their heels or if they have some important meeting to attend. . . . Why would anyone rather look at birds through a gunsight instead of binoculars?

MAY 26

People who find time's swift passage painful cannot bear the sedentary life. In activity they find peace. As the scenery streams past, they feel that time is slowing down. Their lives become a journey that never ends.

The alternative is the hermitage.

I never tire of studying my landscape. My eyes know each nook and cranny there and still explore them eagerly every morning as if discovering them for the first time. I look for three things: fresh nuances in this well-explored tableau, deeper understanding of my remembered idea of the place, confirmation that my move here was a wise decision. Immobility compels me to perform this exercise of virginal observation. If I neglect it, I open the door to the longing to go elsewhere.

One never tires of grandeur: an ancient sedentary principle. And anyway, why complain? Things are not as static as they seem: light fine-tunes beauty, transfigures it. Beauty may be cultivated and renews itself day after day.

Travelers in a hurry need change. The sight of a patch of sunshine on a sandy hillside is not enough for them. Their place is on a train, before a television, but not in a cabin. In the end, along with vodka, bears, and storms, the Stendhal syndrome—or hyperkulturemia, psychosomatic suffocation at the sight of overwhelming beauty—is the only danger threatening the hermit.

MAY 27

It takes me seven hours to toil up a crumbling ridge covered with dwarf pines, spongy lichens, and flakes of schist to gain the summit that crowns my "white valley" at 6,560 feet. On the other side, the verso of my recto world. The other side is, always, a promise. One takes a look at it as if tossing out a net: to cement the certitude of going there one day to look around. Back down from the mountain, we carry that pledge alive in us: a part of our gaze is still up on the mountaintop. . . .

Lying close to each other on the stones at the summit, the dogs stare at the landscape. They are *contemplating* it, I'd

put my hand in a fire on that. Little dogs are "poor in world,"
Herr Heidegger? No, only stripped down to the most accurate
part of their knowledge, completely confident in the moment
and careless of all abstraction. The courage of dogs: to look
straight at what appears before them, without wondering if
things could have been otherwise. I think about men's efforts
to deny all consciousness to animals. Thousands of years of
Aristotelian, Christian, and Cartesian philosophy lock us
into the conviction that an insurmountable divide separates
us from beasts. They lack morality: their actions—even their
altruistic behaviors—are considered devoid of intentional-
ity. They live without any suspicion of their own mortality.
Adapted to their environment, they are incapable of opening
themselves to the whole of reality and will never have any
notion of the world. The animal is merely an impoverished
will, without any representation of its surroundings. Chained
to the immediate, unable to transmit anything, the animal
supposedly deprives itself of History and culture. And the
philosophers keep bashing us over the head with the claim
that no one has ever seen a monkey interpret a natural scene
symbolically or express any esthetic judgment.

    And yet deep in the woods, what we see of animals is
troubling. How can we be certain that a dancing cloud of
midges in the setting sunlight has no meaning? What do we
know about the thoughts of a bear? What if crustaceans bless
the coolness of water without having any way to let us know
this, while we have no hope of ever figuring this out? And how
can we measure the emotions of sparrows when they greet
the dawn from the highest branches? And why shouldn't butterflies in the noonday sun find some esthetic feeling in their
choreography? "The one-year-old bird has no notion of the

eggs for which it builds a nest, or the young spider any idea of the prey for which it spins a web..." (Schopenhauer in *The World as Will and Representation*). But what do you know about that, Arthur? Where did you obtain your information on this subject, from what conversation with which bird do you draw such certainty? My two dogs choose to face the lake, blinking, enjoying the peace of the day, and their drool is a thanksgiving. They are conscious of the happiness of resting there, on the summit, after the long climb. Heidegger tumbles into the water and Schopenhauer as well. Glug-glug, goes thought. I regret that some philosopher schooled in the old humanism (a spiritual masturbation) cannot witness the silent prayer pronounced by two five-month-old pups before a geological fault twenty-five million years old.

Back to the lake. It creaks in the peace of the evening. The ice is saying farewell: no wonder it's moaning.

MAY 28

I spend the day with Delachaux and Niestlé's bird guide: "848 species and 4,000 drawings." This book is a breviary devoted to the ingenuity of life, to the infinite subtleties of evolution, a celebration of style. Even the most sophisticated of urban dwellers for whom birds are stupid robots with crazed eyes, blown hither and yon by the wind, will bow before the audacious livery of the pheasant, the rock ptarmigan, or the ruddy shelduck. I try to identify each of the visitors from the sky. Putting names to plants and animals using field guides is like recognizing superstars in the street thanks to celebrity magazines. Instead of "Ohmigod, it's Madonna!" you exclaim, "Wow, there's a Siberian crane!"

MAY 29

I always go out with a flare gun in my hand in case a bear is roaming the forest. The wilderness begins right outside the door. My home offers no transition: no garden, for example. There is a threshold, of course: a plank, an "air lock" between the civilized world and the perils of the forest. Stags, lynxes, and bears stroll by the cabin; the dogs sleep right outside the door; flies buzz up under the eaves. The two realms are contiguous. The cabin is a tiny island of human survival in this Eden and not an implantation of pioneers determined to improve the earth. During the conquest of Siberia, the tsar's Cossacks built entrenched camps, enclosing a church, an arms depot, and a few buildings behind a palisade of pines trimmed into points at the top. They called such a small fortress an *ostrog*, and these posts protected them from an outside world that had all the time in the world to wait them out. If the Cossacks were there, it was because they dreamed of transforming the taiga, whereas a hermit is content to be dwelling in the forest. The windows serve to welcome nature per se, not to fend it off. The hermit contemplates nature, uses what he needs of it, but cherishes no ambitions to subdue it. The cabin allows him to take a position, but does not enforce a statute. He may play the hermit, but not claim to be a pioneer.

The hermit agrees to be henceforth weightless in the workings of the world, no longer counting as anything in the chain of causality. His thoughts will not influence anyone or affect the course of events. His actions will signify nothing. (Perhaps he may still figure in a few memories.) How light that thought is! And how clearly it foretells the final release: we are never so alive as when we are dead to the world!

*

A russet moon rose tonight, its reflection in the shattered lake ice like a blood-red Host on a wounded altar.

MAY 30

Today I wrote little things on the trunks of some birches. *Birch, I entrust this message to you: go tell the sky I say hello.* Birch bark feels as pleasant to write on with a pen as parchment is. Certain *zeks* recorded their memories on the skin of these trees.

After that, I skipped some stones, and now I'm trying to improve my knife throwing with an old board for a target.

It really is nice to have some free time.

MAY 31

A mountain slope of 5,000 feet extends that much again on its journey down to the bottom of Baikal, and my cabin sits precisely at this halfway point, on a tiny break in a descent just under two miles long. I live balanced between a gulf and a rock face. The river has finally broken the sheath of ice along the shore, opening the sluices. The torrents tumble and frolic all the way to the lake, making the sound of life on its way to a party. The rivers are slashing their way through the forest.

A pair of eiders takes the waters just off the cape. Whenever two sheets of drifting ice threaten to close in on them, they fly off to another open spot. An allegory of exile.

Sometimes my gaze lingers on a stretch of open water on which two ducks then suddenly alight, as if to fulfill a presentiment. As when the eye discovers in a book a phrase for which the mind has long been waiting without ever managing to compose it.

The first capricorn beetles have arrived. They fly heavily through the clearing and plunk down upon the chopping blocks. I feel affection for these insects. Their long, black, backswept antennae frame their jet carapaces. They scramble clumsily over the trunks of the pines. *Love thy neighbor as thyself.* Wouldn't real love be the love of what is irremediably different from us? Not a mammal or a bird, for they are still too close to our humanity, but an insect, a paramecium. Humanism gives off whiffs of a corporatism based on the imperative to love what resembles us. We are supposed to love one another the way the dental surgeon loves other dental surgeons. In the clearing, I reverse the proposition and try to love creatures with an intensity proportional to their degree of biological distance from me. To love is not to celebrate one's own reflection in the face of one's double, but to recognize the value of what one can never know. Loving a Papuan, a child, or one's neighbor is hardly a challenge. But a sea sponge! A lichen! One of those tiny plants roughed up by the wind! Here's what's tough: feeling infinite tenderness for the ant busy rebuilding its hill.

A short afternoon at Middle Cedar Cape to observe the geese sailing around the inland pond. On the way back, I find fresh bear tracks mixed with mine. They weren't there before. The dogs don't react at all. I pass again by the ruins of the refusenik's cabin. Must a man head for the woods at all costs if he rejects his times? There is silence to be found in these secluded vaults.

One can also close one's eyes: the eyelid is the most effective screen between the self and the world.

V.E. down at Zavorotni has often spoken to me about the dissident who lived here, describing him to me as a nice fellow. The idea of this noble soul's existence in harmony with the brutal beauty of these surroundings makes me see this cabin in a friendly light. I imagine the poor guy picking wild onion to flavor his char, talking to the birds, leaving the remains of his fish on the shore for the foxes. It's only in Paris, where I live, that intellectuals cultivate a fascination for bastards and make heroes of criminals. Which is the error denounced by Varlam Shalamov, who survived seventeen years in the Gulag, in his *Essays on the Criminal World*: "every writer seems to have chipped in on this sudden demand for a romanticism of crime, this frenzied poeticizing of thugs...." Criminals are not heroic wolves. And the cabins that have sheltered them do not give off an aura of serenity.

The high pressures building up at the foot of the mountains plunge me into lethargy for the rest of the day. Dreary hours of ennui, rocking in the hammock.

I haven't even the strength to read. I'm dozing beneath a cedar when a rainstorm chases me into the cabin. And then the sight of a steaming cup of tea fills me with an immense feeling of security as the heavens rampage outside. To the west, liquid chaos. Rain was invented so that we can be glad to be under a roof. The dogs are beneath the front door awning. Ideal companions for these moments of withdrawal: vodka and a cigar. They're all that poor people and loners have left. And the health police would like to outlaw these blessings! So that we can die in good shape?

The rain has passed, the air is drying the forest. Through my binoculars I spot a bear standing two or three hundred yards away on the south shore. The bear stays perfectly still.

Then I realize that the boulders are quivering in the evening air: I'm having palpitations over a mirage.

I make some bread. I knead the dough for a long time. Nothing is softer or sweeter to the touch when one is alone. It's easy to understand the wealth of expressions exploring this relationship between flesh and dough. A woman baking things is an aphrodisiac figure, plump and rosy, evoking a healthy eroticism. I eat my bread and force myself not to think anymore about women baking because I still have two months to go, out in this hole.

Tears

JUNE 1

Watching the aerial displays of the ducks and geese, I sit at my table on the beach like one of those judges at a figure-skating competition getting ready to hold up their signs.

Amorous geography: I prefer shingle beaches where people shiver in wool sweaters to those deep-fryer sandy strands littered with oily bodies. Baikal's stony shores fall into the first category.

The plugs of slushy ice blocking the bay for several days have been dispersed by the storm; the wind punished the innocent cabin all night long.

JUNE 2

Zen monks called lingering in bed in the morning "forgetfulness in sleep." My forgetfulness lasts until noon.

I assemble my kayak of blue canvas, but slowly, due to my lack of technical expertise. The instructions say the assembly should take two hours. I put in five, and it's a major victory when I glide out onto the water this evening. With a few strokes of the paddle, I regain what the breakup of the ice had cost me: the possibility of seeing the mountain whole. It has turned green. The larches have gotten dressed again. Up to their chests in water, Aika and Bek, in a panic, can't figure out how to follow me and let out keening moans. Then

Aika realizes that I'll eventually come back to the beach, so they need only run beside the lake in the same direction as I'm paddling.

"Never go more than three hundred feet from shore." This was Volodya's injunction up at Elohin the last time I was there. The lake water is so cold that if you capsize, you will die. No one can survive in 37° F water, and fishermen have drowned here within shouting distance of the shore, even though Jules Verne mentions the legend of this lake in *Michael Strogoff*: "No Russian has ever drowned in Baikal."

There is water, and there are winds. Both are treacherous. Born in the mountains, the *sarma* can awaken in minutes and whip up waves nine feet high. Boats are swept out and overturned. The lake takes payment in men for what they take away in fish: death pays the debt. I learned recently that Volodya lost his son to the lake five years ago, and then I understood why he would spend hours staring out through the clear glass. Sometimes one contemplates a landscape while thinking of the people who once loved it; the atmosphere is steeped in remembrance of the dead.

The dogs slaver their joy when I return to shore. Avian squadrons streak through the sky. Reflections offer the chance to admire Baikal's glory twice over.

JUNE 3

Addressing the young poet Franz Xaver Kappus, Rainer Maria Rilke writes in his letter of February 17, 1903: "If your daily life seems poor, do not blame it, blame yourself that you are not poet enough to call forth its riches. . . ." And here is the American naturalist and essayist John Burroughs, in *The Art of Seeing Things*: "The tone in which we speak to the world is the one the world uses with us. Give your best and you will get the best in return." We alone are responsible for the gloominess of our lives. The world is gray because of our blandness. Life seems pallid? Change your life, head for the cabins. In the depths of the woods, if life remains dreary and your surroundings unbearable, the verdict is in: you can't stand yourself! Make the necessary arrangements.

I spend an hour sawing up the trunk of a dead larch in the clearing. The wood is still viable and the growth rings clearly visible. The sun tints the tree's flesh, making it look appetizing. There are some sights that the human eye has no right to see, as when man exposes to the light things that were not at all prepared to receive it, thus breaking a taboo, changing the writing. In *The Golden Pavilion*, Mishima describes the cross section of a tree that is now open "to the rustling flow of the wind and the sun, for which it was never destined." Cutting down trees, picking flowers: will we one day pay for these tiny liberties that we take with the order of things, these infinitesimal transformations of the initial setup? When one of his disciples suggested to Confucius that irrigation ditches be dug in the kitchen garden, the sage replied, watering can in hand, "Who knows where that would lead us?" The advantage, in a cabin, is that aside from the occasional felling of a tree, one doesn't change much in the general layout.

I'm gliding over silk. The sound of paddles in the silence... The dogs didn't whine when I set out, and they're trotting along to the south. Bek's white coat stands out against the azaleas of the slope. Volodya was no fool: after a quarter hour of caution, I'm boldly cutting between the capes and have wound up more than a mile from shore, sitting in a canvas craft supported by a wooden frame I put together while taking a few liberties with the instructions. I've reached the ice jam that floats way offshore; the frozen chunks clink in the sun. I float perfectly still on the cold oily surface. Two yards from my bow, a seal pokes its head up and stares at me. It has no arms, no legs, but the look in its eyes is something like an old man's, a gaze as deep as its domain. I speak to the seal, which listens, peers at me nearsightedly, and dives.

JUNE 4

Every morning, upon arising, I greet the ducks. More and more of them are arriving at the lake after days of flying up along the 105th meridian east. According to the dictionary of symbols, ducks represent love and fidelity for the Japanese. As for the cedars here, they stand for virginity and purity in European esotericism. My stay is placed under the auspices of virtue.

I owe my presence here to that July day seven or eight years ago when I discovered the shores of Baikal, a first impression that became the certainty that I would one day see them again. Like those followers of the Sufi doctrines espoused by the French intellectual René Guénon, esotericists who are obsessed with finding the Golden Age, we are a few nomadic souls who seek by any means to relive the most intense moments of our existence. For some of us, these moments were in our childhood; for others, they were our first kiss under the local railway trestle, or a feeling of ineffable bliss one summer evening alive with the trilling of cicadas, or a winter's night filled with the rumination of high-minded and generous thoughts. . . . For me, the apex was at the edge of that sandy talus sloping down to Lake Baikal.

Mishima in *The Golden Pavilion*: "What gives meaning to our life's actions is fidelity to a certain moment, and our effort to make that moment last forever...." Everything we undertake to do would flow from an ephemeral and intangible inspiration; a fraction of a second would establish existence. The Buddhists call them satori, these moments when our consciousness glimpses something that disappears forthwith. Blindly, we attempt to recover it, longing to revive that vanished sensation. Days stream by in this fumbling quest; we wander through and throughout our lives. We advance, butterfly net in hand, hoping to catch what has fled. This attempt to relive the satori, thwarted and revived a thousand times, will drive our efforts until death delivers us from the obsessive desire to resuscitate what has fainted away.

Alas, one cannot bathe in the same lakes twice. The satori cannot ever be repeated. A hierophany—a physical manifestation of the sacred, serving as spiritual inspiration—visits us only once. Madeleines cannot be reheated. And the shores of Baikal are now too familiar to me to draw the slightest tear from my eye.

JUNE 5

I paddle to the north, as this afternoon draws to a close, with two fishing rods hooked on the gunwales. The bays spread out beaches of pink shingle. The water's clarity allows glimpses of rocks on which the sun slaps splashes of lagoon brightness. An ice raft slips by with eight seagulls sunning themselves. From out on the lake, I discover the new face of the mountain. The tender green strip of larches supports the greenish-bronze band of cedars coiffed by the bluish-green frieze of the dwarf pines. Surviving patches of granular snow punctuate these lines like commas. The mountains are playing at standing on their heads, and their reflections are even lovelier than the reality. The water's depth and mystery impart vibrancy to the images, and the trembling of the surface conjures visions at the edge of a dream.

As the prow approaches, the ducks barely manage to lift off. I can paddle up to them without frightening them at all. I beach the kayak on a sandy shore where a torrent falls frothing into the lake. A storm chases me under a cedar, where the dogs rejoin me. The lake is like coal-black flannel pricked by a deluge of needles. In five minutes, the sky clears. Beneath the rainbow, wearing waders, I fish in the current. Ducks brush past me. Shafts of sunshine dab the forest with blond highlights. There is a perfect equilibrium in this distribution of roles played by the mountain, the creatures, the water, and the shore.

As if they'd had an appointment, the fish suddenly start biting. In twenty minutes, I catch six char. While the light exhausts itself making holes in the clouds, I lie down on the beach in front of a wood fire, the dogs at my side, the kayak drawn halfway up on shore, and, listening to the music of the waves, I watch my fish grill on skewers of green wood, and I think that life ought always to be like this: an homage rendered by humanity to the dreams of childhood. I struggle against the temptation to take a picture.

The sun, as usual, decides to fling its last light over Buryatia.

JUNE 6

Last night, suffering from insomnia, I went out onto the beach with my flare guns. The moon is waning. She'll be back. Of that we can be sure. You're better off betting on satellites than on messiahs. In the morning, the air is as joyous and flighty as a Dufy painting. The sound of the waves has invaded my life. The swell on the lake is a song of freedom.

From the top of the talus, the trunks of the pines and cedars frame slabs of flat turquoise down on the lake. A long promenade by the azure shore.

The kayak: the shuttle of a loom, plying back and forth on the warp of Baikalian silks.

After paddling around to correct the defective rudder, I pitch my hammock in the clearing. Looking out, I see the watery plain the heavens use as a mirror to try out different tints of light. "I felt a peculiar emotion, observing with what detailed precision earthly things gave refuge to the colors of the sky." Mishima, *The Golden Pavilion*. I read a few of Cicero's letters. The hermit, without access to the news of the day, owes it to himself to be up-to-date on the doings of ancient Rome. In *The Thousand and One Nights*, amid the palms and the opulence, this sentence strikes an unpleasant note: "This generosity you're putting on for me here must surely have a purpose." I prefer this homage to gratuity in *Gilles*, Drieu la Rochelle's novel about the education of a French fascist between the two World Wars: "The less direction his life had, the more sense it made."

JUNE 7

I'm writing at the wooden table; the dogs are sleeping on the warm sand. Everything is quiet, intense, and luminous.

At the edge of the beach, anemones in bloom. Bees and wasps are drinking themselves silly there. Why didn't God, in his infinite wisdom, decree that man would simply and credulously believe in Him, without any fuss or questions? To have invented that perfectly inexplicable thing, the fertilization of flowers by Hymenoptera, and to have forgotten to leave tangible signs of His existence? Gross negligence!

JUNE 8

Barking! I'm up in a flash. In the distance, the sound of an approaching motor. It's five a.m. and a boat is coming from the south. Through the binoculars I recognize one of Sergei's small aluminum craft. Fifteen minutes later, he lands in the company of sad-eyed Yura. The tea kettle is on and I've set yesterday's blini out on the table. When they come in, I'm seated and everything is in order. Sergei can't get over it and talks about "the discipline of people who read." Now there's something that polishes France's reputation on the cheap! The cabin sparkles like a Prussian guard post. Sergei hasn't caught on that without the dogs, I'd still be snoring. I must have been an innkeeper in a previous life; I serve my guests with an eagerness tinged with irritation: an impromptu visit is a disturbance as well as a delight. The two men left Pokoyniki yesterday evening, zigzagged among the islands of rubble ice, and are heading for Elohin. This year they are the first to navigate the lake after the debacle in May. Sergei treats me to a chronicle of the treachery and rancor displayed by the inspectors of the guard posts. The critical theory of the desiccation of the human soul by modernity—formulated by Ralph Waldo Emerson and Jacques Ellul and later taken up by Julien Coupat and others nostalgic for the bonds of community—does not hold up. It isn't crowding in the *urban park* that breeds nastiness, nor is it the stress provoked by market pressures that transforms men into snarling rats, nor is it the mirror-image rivalry of living cheek by jowl that "commands brothers to hate one another" (Coupat in *Tiqqun*). At Baikal, separated by dozens of miles of shoreline, living among the wonders of the woods, men tear one another apart like next-door apartment-house neighbors in a vulgar megapolis. Change the venue, and the nature of the "brothers" will stay the same. The peacefulness of the setting won't mean a thing. Man can't remake himself in a different image.

Sergei pays me the best compliment of my life: "Your presence here puts off the poachers. You'll have saved four or five bears." We lubricate these courtesies with a bottle of vodka. Yura, feeling unsociable, says nothing, doesn't drink, and hangs back, now and then dispatching an onion or a smoked fish. The two men take off for Elohin, where they have things to do, and we arrange to meet that evening at Zavorotni, where they'll be spending the night.

We've emptied the bottle, but fifteen miles in a kayak will put paid to any migraine. I paddle slowly, dawdling in the bays. I move at an otter's pace, and the prow slices through hours of silence. Bek and Aika are a little black dot and a little white dot at the mouths of the torrents. A marsh-hawk studies me from the top of an ash tree. The mergansers cackle. I cut across the capes a little over a mile from their shores. Six hours later, Zavorotni. Sergei, Yura, and a few fishermen are sitting by a fire in front of the large *izba* belonging to their friend V.M.

The lake is falling asleep, the animals calm. Until three in the morning, we feed the fire, swallow smoked fish, and empty bottles. I would have liked to collapse in the warmth of a cabin. Russia has taught me never to count on the slightest respite after any effort and always to be prepared to trash myself with vodka after having worn myself out mile after mile.

One of the fishermen, Igor, can't hold his liquor. He gives off in sobs what he absorbs in ethanol and collapses in my arms blubbering over the child that isn't on the way. I'll remember all my life his big tears in a night still echoing with the cries of seagulls. He and his wife have consulted a shaman specializing in fertility and now want to go stay in Tibetan temples where the power of bodhisattvas could make them fruitful. I don't dare console him by pointing out that the human anthill is about to explode. And that the French anthropologist Claude Lévi-Strauss described our billions of humans as meal worms in an overcrowded habitat in which we're killing ourselves with our own toxins. And that the old master, worried about the demographic pressures now afflicting the Earth, had forbidden himself to make "any prediction about the future"—he who'd been born in a world six times less densely populated. And that in his play *The Dead Queen*, the novelist and playwright Montherlant put these words in the mouth of the king when he discovers that his daughter-in-law is pregnant: "My God, will it never end?" And that tossing an infant into the lions' cage is not, perhaps, the wisest thing to do. And that the desire to be a father is easily thwarted by maintaining a small fund of pessimism.

JUNE 9

I brought along Chateaubriand's *Life of Rancé,* about the founder of the Trappists, and I'd planned on spending a pleasant day at Zavorotni with this master of the hermit's way of life, but feeling guilty about leaving the sun to go on its way alone, I wound up parading my hangover in the noonday sun on the schist slag of the abandoned mine here. Up until the collapse of the Soviet Union, "free men" gutted the mountain in search of microcrystalline quartzite, leaving behind what is known in Russia as a serpentine, an eighteenth-century French word for a road with hairpin turns. This one is littered with the carcasses of engines and Caterpillar excavators. My clothes are in rags, my hair is every which way, I've got booze breath and jaundiced eyes, and even the dogs look pitiful, done in by yesterday's marathon. We all three collapse at regular intervals along the road to recharge ourselves in the sunshine. At an elevation of 3,280 feet, we reach the break in the slope created by the umbilical edge of a glacier long ago. The amphitheater chewed from the mountain by machines has the dreary look common to all derelict mines. I climb to 6,560 feet, spitting out the scoria of my long night. Up there, the view of the hidden part of the lake is an invitation to adventure. Life is about moving forward, and there's defeat in retracing one's steps. We stagger back down through the couloirs of soft snow. Our bodies didn't need to climb up almost 5,000 feet of crappy roadway today. I ought to have read Chateaubriand while drinking black tea and admiring the ballet of eiders whipping up the good black cream of the lake.

At ten this evening, surrounded by his dogs, V.E. serves me supper in his home, which is more like a kennel than an *izba*. The floor is sticky with grease, and the stove features huge simmering vats of seal offal and trimmings from elk quarters: dog food. It looks like an athanor, the furnace of an alchemist in eighth-century Lotharingia.

"So, the mine?" asks V.E.

"Very pretty, up there," I reply.

"The dogs?"

"They followed me, the scamps."

"Before, this village was alive; we had a little restaurant. Today, a ruin."

"Tovarishch, you're pining for the Soviet Union."

"No: nostalgia is pining only for your youth."

JUNE 10

V.E. serves me braised seal for breakfast. This meat is a nuclear explosion in the mouth that sends its strength all through the body.

"Comrade," I announce, "give me some seal, hand me a tank, and leave Poland to me!"

"That's not a Russian proverb."

"It could be."

"Yeah."

For the moment my friend is feeding his ten dogs with the ingenuity of a wrestler. He has to invade the barking heap with his pail and hurl the rations into the pans while beating back the onslaught of the dogs. Mine are pretty much holding their own in the melee. Whoever doesn't fight doesn't eat.

On the trip home, I bless the seal meat for giving me its

strength. A contrary wind and a heavy chop cost me seven hours of effort to cover about fifteen miles. The dogs wait up for me with short siestas on the smooth boulders. My muscles are in shreds. Dehydration probably has something to do with it. Russia makes its drunks live like athletes. The shore creeps along. Seals keep popping up.

I take a break: a nap ashore with the dogs on the warm rocks, near a fire hot enough to drive spiders from their lairs.

At five I land on my beach just when a trawler arrives to nudge its steel prow among the rocks. The captain asks me if a couple of Dutch passengers may come ashore for a moment.

Erwin works on Sakhalin Island for an oil company. His wife speaks perfect French. The two children are sunburned and better behaved than my dogs. The cabin must seem like a dream to them: Snow White's cottage, and in it, one of the seven dwarfs. We drink tea in a very civilized way, standing on the beach. They stay fifteen minutes and take a photo, which you would do if you weren't staying six months.

At the top of the gangplank, Erwin calls out, "I've got a *Herald Tribune*. Want it?"

"Sure!"

"It's last week's."

"Doesn't matter."

He tosses me the paper and it occurs to me that it's well worth having lived thirty-eight years to have a Batavian guy on a Russian fishing boat deliver the *Herald Tribune* to me out in the taiga.

The news: little Afghan girls abused by their relatives, then repudiated by their mothers. Women whipped by mullahs (photo). Iraqi Shiites blowing up Sunnis along with a few of their own in the process because homemade IEDs are tricky (photo). The Turks recall their diplomats from Israel (commentary). Iranian atomic scientists crowing over making great strides with their programs. By page four, I'm thinking I wouldn't mind staying a few months more out here. The newsprint of the *Herald* works quite nicely to wrap Siberian fish.

JUNE 11

Rancé is the St. Anthony of the temperate latitudes. One of God's fools minus the sand dunes and scorpions. It's the seventeenth century: a man of wealth and distinction decides to die to the world. At the age of thirty-seven, he sets a new course for the wilderness "without memory and without resentment." Chateaubriand paints a frightening portrait of Rancé. Giving no warning, he leaves his gilded halls, renouncing his aristocratic life for one of penitence. Taking the Gospels literally, he pays his debt to the poor and then, in the hills of Perche in northern France, founds *l'ordre de La Trappe*, a congregation of deadly serious discipline, a "Christian Sparta." In his retreat, he prays, writes, meditates, and mortifies his sick body. He will live thirty-seven more years in solitude, crippled by suffering, cloistered in the "desolation" of stones. Thirty-seven years of pleasure against thirty-seven years of silence: a loan redeemed. With the maniacal exactitude of an accountant, Rancé will repay the debt he owed the devil, drawing "his last strength from his first weakness." In a letter to the Bishop of Tournai, he sums everything up: "We live to die." His flight fascinates and repels me in equal measure. His extremism dazzles me, his motive shocks and disgusts me. In the abbé's anxieties, there is something of the feverish child who exclaims to the heavens: "I want the absolute and I want it *now!*"

The impulsive impatience is superb, but the fire is morbid, devouring everything that lies outside an expectation of the afterlife. Out on the taiga, I would rather gather up moments of felicity than intoxicate myself with the absolute. The scent of azaleas delights me more than that of incense. I beam at fresh blossoms instead of at a silent sky. As for the rest—simplicity, austerity, oblivion, renunciation, and indifference to comfort—I admire and willingly imitate that.

JUNE 12

This morning, fog. The world wiped out. It's weather for water sprites. When the cottony mist dissipates, I set out to fish the river at North Cedar Cape. Fishing: you gain a fish but lose some time. Worth it?

I let the flies drift along the current and keep them suspended in the water, about four or five feet below the surface, where the fish gather to glean the nutritious outfall from the rivers. The thrill when the cork takes a dive: dinner will be served! When I kill a char, shivers run over its skin as life leaves in electrical discharges. The skin then loses its luster. Life is what gives us color.

JUNE 13

In *Life of Rancé*, this quotation from the *Elegies* of Tibullus: "How sweet it is while lying in bed to hear fierce winds." The wind rampages all day long, and I read my Tibullus.

JUNE 14

The lashing surf has washed the rocks. I advance carefully, trying not to slip. The dogs are afraid of the waves, which have teeth so they can bite the earth. The points of the capes are hidden by flying foam. The wind is still carrying on in the dark forest; the taiga crackles. The occasional gull shoots by. Millions of flies have hatched out on the shingle, covering entire sections of beach. The dogs lick them up. The flies live only a week, and the animals love them: free protein and easy pickings. The sand is starred with plantigrade tracks: flat-footed bears have come down to the feast.

The dogs can't manage to cross the Lednaya River. Aika has jumped onto a rock in the middle of the current and waits for me to come wading though the churning water to get her. Bek wails pitifully, convinced that we're plotting to desert him. I cross again to ferry him over on my shoulders. To get past the abrupt shoreline north of the river, I go up onto slopes littered from landslides. These cliffs and their way of murmuring: "Hey sweetie, come on over here. . . ." The wind's nasty humor gives me wings.

I reach my goal: a cascading torrent of a river almost two miles north of the Lednaya. A good spot for fish but three hours away. The dogs nose around for a moment, then go to sleep under the awnings of the rhododendrons. I admire the ease with which they collapse at the slightest respite. My new motto: In all things, do as a dog does! Bionics takes its inspiration from biology and applies it to technology. We need a school of ethobionics that would use animal behavior to guide our actions. At the moment of decision, instead of seeking counsel from our heroes—what would Marcus Aurelius,

Lancelot, or Geronimo have done?—we would ask ourselves, "And now, what would my dog decide? Or a horse? Or a tiger? Or even an oyster (a model of placidity)?" Bestiaries would provide our rules of conduct. Ethology—the scientific study of animal behavior—would become a moral science. I interrupt my reverie when a char pulls my cork down after him. This evening I bring four fish back to the cabin. And I wolf them down, because that's what animals do.

JUNE 15

These rock flies: they flow down cliffs and tree trunks in silky streams. They are sacred manna. The month of June when the animals need all their vigor for love presents a problem in the cycle of life. How to bridge the gap between the awakening in May and the abundance of July? Nature has come up with—the flies. These poor insects serve as fodder destined to provide energy during a period of penury. In two weeks, their job done, they will vanish after a brief existence, sacrificed in the common biological interest. They don't forget to live, though: at the slightest touch of sunlight, they go into Brownian motion, quivering with the lightest of vibrations, and mate. Their trembling reminds me of the shiver of a secret joy, and I like them so much that I almost sprain my ankles trying not to crush them on the rocky beaches.

JUNE 16

Everything has collapsed. On the satellite phone I save for emergencies and have not yet used to make any calls, five lines appear, more painful than a searing burn. The woman I love has dismissed me. She has lost interest in a man who's like a straw in the wind. I've sinned through my flights, my evasions, and this cabin.

After being gone for years, she came back to me when I was just leaving on that first assignment for Lake Baikal. Now she's the one leaving me, and I'm looking at those same shores. For three hours, I wander along the beach. I've let happiness fly away. Life should be nothing but this: giving constant thanks to fate for the slightest blessing. *Being happy* is *knowing* that you are.

It's five in the afternoon. The pain comes in waves; at times I find some relief. I manage to feed the dogs, even to fish. But the ache always returns, with a life of its own: molten lead coursing through my being.

I dream about a little house in the suburbs with a dog, wife, and children, protected by a row of fir trees. For all their narrowness, the bourgeoisie has nevertheless understood this essential thing: we must give ourselves the possibility of a minimum of happiness.

I'm condemned to stay in this dead end full of stupid ducks, face to face with my pain.

I have to marshal my strength to make it to the next hour. I bury myself in a book. As soon as I stop reading, I hear those five lines in the sat-phone message shrieking through my skull.

I close the book and cry into my dogs' fur. I had no idea that fur soaks up tears so well. On human skin, tears slide away. Usually the dogs are capering all over at this hour; tonight, their heads hanging a little, they keep quiet under my miserable flood of weeping. I have only a flare gun with which to blow my brains out. And no guarantee of success. A seal appears above the waterline, just in front of the beach. . . . I tell myself that it's her, come to smile at me. I must manage to speak to her one last time. You're always late to your own life; time doesn't hand out second chances. Life can ride on one roll of the dice. And me, I hared off to the forest, leaving her behind.

I read until I'm worn out, because if my eyes look away from the page, the pain chokes me and forces me to get up. Tonight I keep hearing boats, but it's the throbbing of my eyes.

JUNE 17

I'm padlocked into this Eden I made for myself. The sky is blue yet black. Strange how time withdraws its friendship from you. Just yesterday, it slipped by like satin. Now every second needles me.

To be thirty-eight years old and here, by a lake, crawling and asking a dog why women go away.

Without Aika and Bek, I'd be dead. This afternoon I chop wood from four thirty to six thirty, until I can't hold the ax anymore. "Only the purest of heart can become murderous because of others," writes Jim Harrison in *Dalva*. The wave comes back. Tears are kept in check by reading. In films, wolves retreat before the flames of torches.

I scuttled the ship of my life and realized it when the water was up to the gunwales. Question: It's seven o'clock; how do I make it to eight? It's a lovely evening, with pompadour clouds that are a little silly, like those velvet tassels on old-lady curtains. The fish surface and kiss the wavelets, leaving circles that grow larger, fade away.

I scribble all day in my little black notebooks. Writing anything at all so as not to feel pain. The notebooks: the people inside them are full of memories, anecdotes, thoughts. I read *The Stoics*: there are things in their practices you can use to steel yourself, a first step toward consolation. I'd like to snuff out my pain in this forest that knows nothing of sorrow. Life everywhere: ducks, seals, and a bear, in my binoculars, at the base of the hill where I like to rest. It's the evening hour when everyone goes home and says a last thank-you to this latest day of life.

My body is compressed with suffering. Can the great pressures of grief provoke congestive heart failure?

The only hope on the horizon is the expected arrival tomorrow of Bertrand de Miollis and Olivier Desvaux, two painter friends who are traveling in Russia and have promised to visit me. Sergei is supposed to bring them here by boat. As it turns out, they're arriving right when I'm as flat as a tar blotch on a beach.

I'll say nothing to them, hide my tears, and use their presence to stay alive.

JUNE 18

Hang on. And to hang on, take strength from the infinite solidity of the little dogs. Nature is overjoyed at getting its hands on a new summer. At six in the evening, the sound of an engine rouses me from my stupor. A black dot to the south: my deliverance. I welcome Miollis and Desvaux like a benediction; they will distract me from my *danse macabre*. Sergei heads back without even tossing back a single glass, because the wind is rising. I sit the two painters down at the wooden table beside the lake and unpack all the provisions they've brought from Irkutsk: wine, beer, vodka, hard cheese. We get falling-down drunk. The alcohol takes its toll on our bodies, but at least it chases away all sorrow.

JUNE 19

The happiness lasts one second. There's a pleasant moment upon awakening at dawn, just before consciousness remembers and the heartache begins.

Since the apocalypse of June 16, I've read two Shakespearean comedies, *The Handbook* of Epictetus, the *Meditations* of Marcus Aurelius, José Giovanni's *The Adventurers*, and *Eve*, a psychological thriller by James Hadley Chase, the hero of which is a lousy creep whose character sucks the life out of everything and creates a desert around him. That guy is me. Guided by a mysterious impulse, my hand selected the books I needed to read. Marcus Aurelius helped me. Giovanni showed me the man I should have been; Chase showed me as I am. Books are more useful than psychoanalysis; they say everything, better than life does. In a cabin, mixed with solitude, they make a perfect lytic cocktail, gradually relieving the symptoms of acute disease.

The vodka hangover hangs us out to dry. Miollis and Desvaux emerge at noon, having slept on the cabin floor. To sweat out the poison, we set off on foot for the Lednaya and have lunch on one of the grassy shelves on the cliffs of the right bank. The dogs run around chasing ducks. All that joy!

Two easels planted on a beach before white-smocked painters, who compose their pictures with careful little brushstrokes. A couple of dogs lie at their feet in the pale mauve twilight of Siberia. It's a classically peaceful scene, and I can't take my eyes off my friends, who have been traveling through Siberia painting from nature in the purest tradition of the itinerant painters of Holy Russia. With the help of light and a dollop of time, they create space in two dimensions. I'm writing these lines while they put the finishing touches on their canvases. The cabin is beginning to look like an artist's studio: a Villa Medici for muzhiks.

JUNE 20

At dawn, I pose, sitting at my work table. The two painters have set up their easels in the cabin. Miollis looks like a German troubadour and Desvaux, a Swiss shepherd. Desvaux is technically conservative, painstaking, and generous, and he always pulls something off. Miollis is more hit-and-miss, sometimes blowing his picture but occasionally coming up with a stunner. This morning they are painting a man with a crumpled heart. It's easy to hide feelings. Constructed in haste by Russian government ministers out in the countryside (or so the story goes), "Potemkin villages" were just facades restored and repainted on the fly to hide hovels and impress the ruler of Russia on a tour of inspection, who then went happily home to the palace.

Cheerful Miollis and gentle Desvaux distract me from my misery. Without them, grief would eat me up like a crab.

In one day my guests paint the cabin, the dogs, the beach. It takes as much nerve to try rendering the beauty of this place on canvas as it does to capture it in a few perfectly chosen words.

JUNE 21

This morning, a big ship passes well out on the lake. Ten minutes later the wake reaches the beach, carrying with it something of the world's unpleasant intrusion onto my pristine little property.

The painters spend the day limning the flight of wild geese through the radiant heavens. They stand before their easels as if before a window that is waiting for them to invent its view.

I climb to the top of the crumbling butte to have lunch. Having reached the summit, my dogs gaze pensively at the lake, panting and drooling. Five days ago, these little creatures held out their paws and saved me from drowning.

At twilight, fishing. Desvaux catches dinner for three people and two dogs. His silhouette stands out against the great ash tree that leans over the water at the point of the cape. Unwilling to come down from the heights, the light clings to the spurs of the cliffs. A flash of silver at the end of the line: the lake is giving up its treasures. Writing, painting, fishing: three ways of paying one's respects to time.

JUNE 22

Pollen has fallen on the lake and hems the beaches with bright yellow ribbons. Dead butterflies drift on the waters. Seals keep surfacing to stare at the shore, checking to see that the world is still in its place and that they've done well to dwell in the depths.

Not a sound, not one noise, just the odd butterfly.

"Silence, the ornament of sacred solitudes" (*Life of Rancé*).

Miollis and Desvaux go from painting to painting, offerings in harmony with the genius loci. The infinite superiority of a painting to a photograph. A *snapshot* immobilizes a precise moment in time and stakes it out in two dimensions. (Primitive peoples were not entirely wrong to see photos as thefts.) A *painting* offers a historical interpretation of a moment that will live a long time in the eye of those who contemplate it, and, as a work that does not interrupt the flow of time, its very confection is fluid, inscribed in a long period of composition.

JUNE 23

Shortly before dawn, we head out for a six-hour trek along the shore.

Miollis and Desvaux are returning to Irkutsk and must take a boat setting out this morning from Zavorotni, a fifteen-mile hike from the cabin. We look like three Jewish painters fleeing along the Vistula with all our art impedimenta crammed into beggars' bags. We're bent double under enormous backpacks stuffed with fifty-odd pounds of gouache paints and mediums in tubes, an encyclopedia of Russian painting, and the easels on top. At Middle Cedar Cape, we salute the hermit's ghost. Near the pond by the derelict cabin, we find the carcass of a bear. Leaning against an immense ash tree at South Cedar Cape, an anthill teems with life: millions of skeletons busily build themselves a body. Barnacle geese speed north fast enough to dislocate their necks. I waste some time trying to find the old geologists' path V.E. told me about that runs along some five hundred feet above the lake, but the trail has been invaded by saplings that make walking even more difficult than on the stones of the lakeshore.

At Zavorotni, Miollis and Desvaux leap onto the boat, whose diesel engines we had heard warming up a good hour before arriving at the dock. We've barely time to shake hands. I like this kind of farewell; it's like taking a tumble.

That evening, Sergei, sad-eyed Yura, and Sasha of the missing fingers arrive in Zavorotni by boat. We prepare a feast of smoked fish, nalim liver, caviar with wild onion, and grilled venison.[12] Sasha pours us his homemade rotgut. These Russians have a way of tossing back their drinks and grabbing hunks of meat that displays their pride in bypassing all commercial resources. They live exclusively off the forest, and taking what you need from the woods guarantees contentment. Such men operate autonomously in the order of things but remain bound to the traditions of their fathers, and they are worlds away from the freethinkers who have thrown off all ties to God and princes but depend on cities and their services for food, warmth, and transportation. Who is right? The autarkic muzhik who commends his soul to heaven but never sets foot in a store? Or the modern atheist, liberated from all spiritual corsetry but forced to live on the tit of the system and obey all injunctions imposed by life in society? Must one kill God but submit to legislators, or live free in the forest while still fearing the spirits? Practical and material autonomy doesn't seem a less noble achievement than spiritual and intellectual autonomy. In *On Democracy in America*, in the chapter "What Type of Despotism Democratic Nations Have to Fear," Tocqueville writes: "One forgets that it is above all in the details that it proves dangerous to enslave men. For my part I would be inclined to believe liberty less necessary in great things than in the lesser ones." This evening, emptying bottles with the woodsmen of the taiga, I take sides. For the gods, princes, and beasts, and against the penal code!

"We're taking you home!" exclaims Sergei suddenly. And we throw ourselves into an activity at which Russians excel: raising a toast, breaking camp in a hurry, tossing baggage into a boat, and taking off full speed for no matter where. No matter where—as long as the wind blows, the world is pitching and rolling, and inebriation carries the day with the promise of finding something new at the end of the journey.

There's nowhere more propitious for meditation than an aluminum boat en route across a fog-shrouded lake. Sometimes the edge of a cliff manages to tear the curtain of mist; sections of shore appear and melt away again. I hate *manifestations*. Except when they are revelations of beauty. Our journey resembles thought: the mind proceeds though cotton wadding until a sudden breakthrough permits a glimpse of something. Floating in formlessness, we see the light and can put a name to the shadows.

Sergei cuts the engine and we down a glass in the humid silence. We've been drinking for hours and are soused. Sprawled over the gas cans and fishing nets, sucking on my cigarette, heading through fog in a boat with a drunken captain, I feel reassured. Having lost my lover, I have nothing more to lose. Misfortune casts off ties. Happiness is an obstacle to serenity. When I was happy, I was afraid of unhappiness.

JUNE 24

Throughout Midsummer Day, the sky puts on a superb show. The foehn, that warm, dry wind arising in the lee of a mountain range, caps the summits with clouds and covers the forest with mist as gently as if veiling the amours of shameless animals.

In the hammock, I study the shapes of the clouds. Contemplation is what clever people call laziness to justify it in the eyes of the supercilious, who watch to ensure that we all "find our place in an active society."

JUNE 25

Another day of looking at the sky. Swarms of insects in the gold-dust sunlight. Later, a salmon-colored moon swims up the current of the night to go lay its single monstrous egg in a nest of clouds. Simply put: there's a full and blood-red moon.

JUNE 26

The wrenching sight of drowned butterflies: hundreds of them floating on the lake, some of them still strong enough to struggle. I transform my kayak into a rescue patrol boat and delicately collect the insects one by one. Poor sky flowers fallen on the field of honor. . . . Soon thirty butterflies decorate my blue boat with limp stars. I'm the captain of an ark for Hymenoptera.

JUNE 27

I reach Elohin, with the wind at my back. Stormy weather is on the way, dashing all hopes of sun. Elohin takes on its dismal outpost look. I have an appointment with Mikhail Hippolitov, a preserve inspector who has promised to take me along on his visit to a cabin a day's march beyond the peaks. At noon, in a high wind, bowlegged under the weight of fifty-some pounds of vodka and canned goods, I toil along behind Hippolitov as he trots over the taiga. We ascend the forested slopes above the promontory of Elohin. Hippolitov takes off like a cannonball, slows, announces brief halts, leaps to his feet, and winds up 650 feet above me. Below the pass, at 4,265 feet, pummeled by gusts of rain, my friend requires tea. The situation becomes very Russian: lying beneath low-hanging pine branches, we wait for our tiny fire to heat a pint of water amid the slabs of schist.

Two saddles covered with graphite pebbles open in the ridge, allowing access to a high, marshy plateau. The wind rises, and we wait out a violent squall, huddling behind a rocky projection. It's a voluptuous feeling, walking for miles over springy lichen. You'd almost dream of becoming a herbivore. Partridges squawk at our passing. Centuries of wind have shaped the dwarf pines into labyrinths as tangled as viscera. Strands of moss drip from trees. In the boggy areas, gravity has weighed more heavily on the vegetation than any tropism toward the sky. Crossing into a valley we find a thousand-year-old cedar that goes back before the time of the Mongols. We pass forests of firs, crystalline streams, mountain "shelves" infested with insects, and sloughs where our boots sink deeply into the mud. GPS N 54°36.106'/E 108° 34.491' brings us to Hippolitov's cabin, built two years earlier right on the border of the nature preserve. It's ten feet by ten feet, a haven constructed on the flank of a valley through which winds a river. A conical mountain bristling with evergreens forms the horizon. Wild onion, rhubarb, and bear's garlic grow plentifully nearby, well guarded by swarms of mosquitoes. It's the kind of place I like: an area apart where the evening light falls more softly than elsewhere, as if from pity.

Mikhail plays the host: a salad of wild greens dressed with mayonnaise, along with lard soup and some pepper vodka. From my pack I pull a three-liter bottle of beer that we drink dry before it even has a chance to go *pffft*.

JUNE 28

We walk up a valley clotted with vegetation. And we're staggering like two drunks who've decided to climb a mountain pass after hitting a bar. Every step is a triumph over a cascade of stones, a tangle of roots, or a mini-quagmire. The river flows on indifferently, having a long way to go before reaching the Arctic Ocean via the Lena. At 4,000 feet, the forest leaves the task of masking the rocks to the dwarf pines. Faithful to the Russian principle whereby there can be no excuse—not war, not exodus—for skipping teatime, we spend an hour coaxing fire from a few soaking-wet twigs. Stretched out in a puddle, sipping tepid water in the rain, we have a pleasant conversation.

"Your books are translated?"

"A few of them."

"Into what?"

"Finnish, Italian, German."

"Russian?"

"No."

"That figures; we're still a primitive people."

We have to force our way through clumps of flowering rhododendrons. The pass turns out to feature a small swamp. The rain falls harder. Hippolitov suggests that we turn around, but I don't see myself scramming back through the algal forest to spend the rest of the day in a soggy sleeping bag. We climb slopes that lead to a plateau of "endemic tundra." The lichen here is springier than a nouveau-riche Muscovite's wall-to-wall carpet. Four wild reindeer graze near some old snow, and we try to skulk Comanche-like around them. A hundred yards from the animals, hidden by a rhododendron, we realize that we are not the only skulkers: a brown bear is making an approach and, spotting us, freezes. The impression of competing with a bear at feeding time is not enjoyable. I get my flare gun ready and Hippolitov loads his rifle. The sharp sound of the breech startles the reindeer, which scatter, and the bear must be cursing us but never moves a muscle. Until he stands up on his hind legs. We have to wait a few seconds to find out whether he'll about-face or charge us. That day, no need to shoot: we stare a long time at the gentle undulation, showing over the bushes, of fur in flight.

It takes us two hours to relocate the tributary along which we descended yesterday. Hippolitov has a plan. A year ago, he brought a cast-iron stove that far and would like me to get it the rest of the way to his cabin. Which costs me another two hours of fun carrying sixty-five pounds of stove, two lower corners of which dig into my back while two upper ones catch on branches, provoking with each step a truly bracing flood of chilly water. I must look like those Himalayan porters who cart the most incongruous objects through the Nepalese jungles: leather trunks, mahogany gramophones, tubs for the officers' baths. . . .

JUNE 29

If I'm ever launched in a space capsule, I'll already know what it's like to spend an entire day lying on a cot next to a galactic traveling companion. I'd brought along Kierkegaard's *Sickness unto Death*, which I would not recommend to anyone confined to a cabin by rain. Hippolitov's little radio sputters a constant stream of pop songs and information about the 1941–1945 war. Rain falls from a sky utterly lacking in imagination.

"Mikhail."

"What?"

"We're not having any luck with the rain."

"But it means fewer mosquitoes."

"There's that."

Hippolitov has forgotten his book back in Elohin and stares haggardly at the ceiling as though it were about to start showing a marvelous movie. At four in the afternoon, in a burst of feverish activity, we replace the old stove with the new one, and in the fine warmth it gives off, we dispatch three little glasses of vodka in the traditional salute to "the first smoke." At six, the rain slows to drizzle and we set out to climb the pyramidal peak on the eastern edge of the valley. The rain returns as we get under way. The lichen curtains are liquid veils. The mosses swallow our boots. The mosquitoes can't find space to fly in. It takes us an hour to ascend the thousand feet of uneven terrain crowned with three-hundred-year-old cedars. The trees look like ruins. Around the edges of what was once a bear's den, the little wine-colored bells of wild orchids bring a touch of joy to that world.

I'm awakened in the night by a mouse that's gotten into my sleeping bag, which isn't as scary as a spider—nor as nice as a Kirov ballerina.

JUNE 30

On the streets of Irkutsk, Hippolitov would pass for a proper family man with graying hair and a staid, orderly life. Every year, he spends a few months in the forest, alone, visiting his six cabins, strung along a line seventy miles long, and reconnecting with that conviction certain Russians have that city life must be only an interlude to life in the woods.

We head back. It's still raining. The spellbound bushes seem to be dreaming of Thailand. With my hood pulled tight, I recall my climbs in the fragrant limestone hills of Provence. Walking in the rain, a factory for memories.

In tropical jungles, heat and humidity foster a profusion of life, but growth in the taiga doesn't benefit from such a biological incubator. Whereas the hot jungle is in constant production, the taiga preserves. Here plant growth is slow, but decomposition doesn't clear out the understory as quickly as it does in the lower latitudes. A Siberian cedar can take years to rot. In both cases, vegetable chaos encumbers the ground, the result of tropical exuberance elsewhere and of biostasis here. The cold jungle is a plant museum; the hot jungle, a chlorophyllian laboratory.

In Elohin, my little dogs are waiting, and I have lunch with Volodya, Irina, and Hippolitov: blini with char caviar. There's never enough caviar. But much too much vodka.

Then, with great spoon-scoops into the coffee-colored lake, I scoot off home.

✟✟✟✟✟✟✟✟✟✟✟✟✟✟✟✟✟✟✟✟✟✟✟✟✟✟✟✟✟✟✟✟✟

Peace

JULY 1

A day of fishing. A piscivore, drawing nourishment from a lake, undergoes a psychophysiological transformation. His cells feed on phosphorus, and his character absorbs the essence of the fish. What he loses in red-blooded strength he gains in placidity, taciturnity, dexterity, competence, and restraint.

I catch eight char. The frightened eyes of fish, as if they'd seen forbidden things.

Aika and Bek steal three of my catch. I can't even bring myself to scold them. If I were raising kids, they'd wind up juvenile delinquents.

JULY 2

The air is loaded with bugs. A rumbling hum begins with the first glimmers of light and never falters until nighttime. Beetles crawl along the beams in the cabin, and the capricorns among them colonize my shelves. Gadflies with nightmarish eyes torment the dogs. If these insects weighed ten or twenty pounds, as they did in the Carboniferous period, we'd be a lot less full of ourselves.

JULY 3

Spring, the opening of the floodgates.

The waterfall is flowing free again.

Atop the 160-foot rock wall, water escapes via even the slightest gulley, covering the schist with rushing white streamers. Thanks to some acrobatics along a winding mountain track that cuts its way up to the summit, I reach the head of the falls and the vertiginous vision of this clear mountain cascade plunging into the void.

In the evening, the dogs fight. Their jaws snap like the clashing of sabers. This gray beach: could there ever be a more beautiful place in which to witness a samurai battle, or wander in search of a word, or recite a poem? I live at the edge of a wood, before a vast plain of water, on the rim of a submerged cliff line rooted 5,000 feet underwater and rising 6,500 feet into the sky. All these spaces meet at the cabin.

JULY 4

Luxury? Twenty-four hours at my complete disposal each and every day, for the fulfillment of my slightest desire. The hours are tall girls of shining white standing in the sunlight to serve me. If I want to spend two days on my cot reading a novel, who's to stop me? If I feel like taking off at twilight into the forest, who will dissuade me? The solitary woodsman has two loves, time and space. The first he uses as he pleases; the second he knows through and through.

I stay in my hammock in the broiling sun (72° F!). When I write on the beach, the dogs amble over to flop down at my feet: the Baikalian version of an Irish-country-house spaniel, dozing while his mistress reads.

Long wisps of mist are drifting seductively across the lake.

JULY 5

The insects react with the sensitivity of a seismograph to the faintest rise in temperature. As soon as the air reaches 37° F, they hatch by the millions and churn the air in frenzied flight. The copulation of the capricorn beetles: the antennae touch lightly and the insects make love in statuesque immobility. I wouldn't mind the visit of a young female Slovenian entomologist interested in studying this phenomenon. The ducks, well, they evoke the stability of the bourgeois ménage, gliding in their Sunday best, two by two, nodding discreetly to the other couples. . . .

The world that I inhabit every day, from the clearing to the water's edge, conceals treasures. In the grass, under the sand, armies are on the move. Their soldiers are jewels. They wear varnished armor, golden carapaces, malachite tunics, or striped livery. Walking at North Cedar Cape, I never suspect that I'm treading on gems, cameos, diamonds. Some of them spring from the imagination of a Jugendstil jeweler, inspired by nature's wonders and collaborating with a Faustian alchemist to bring brooches and enamels to life as they emerge from the oven.

Respecting insects brings joy. Taking a passionate interest in the infinitely small helps guard against an infinitely mediocre life. For the insect lover, a puddle can be Lake Tanganyika, a pile of sand takes on the aspect of the Taklamakan Desert, and a patch of brush becomes the Mato Grosso Plateau. Entering the geography of the insect gives grass the dimensions of a world.

JULY 6

When the lake is as slick as oil, the reflection is so pure that you could misread which half of the mirror image is which. My paddles send their echo cleanly to the forest. The reflection is the echo of the image; the echo is the image of the sound.

I catch a six-and-a-half-pound char. I read Bachelard's philosophical reverie, *The Psychoanalysis of Fire*, by my own fire. A mist straight out of a Japanese print invades the shore, "beautiful like the ineffable, changeable like a dream, fleeting like love" (Bachelard).

JULY 7

Insomnia. Regrets and discouragement are dancing a witches' Sabbath in my skull. Sunrise shoos away the bats at four-thirty, and I fall asleep at last.

Is it fatigue? When I get up at noon, I'm floating in a gentle daze. The prospect of happiness: a day that will bring me nothing new. No one on the horizon, no task to accomplish, no need to satisfy, no greeting to return. Eventually a few evening reverences to the seal and a squadron of eiders.

The cabin is *a sidestep*, where one can step aside. The haven of emptiness where no one is forced to *react* to everything. How to measure the comfort of these days free of all obligation to *answer* questions? I can now perceive the aggressive character of a conversation. Claiming to be interested in you, an interlocutor shatters the halo of silence, invades the shore of time, and calls upon you to answer his questions. All dialogue is a battle.

Nietzsche in *Ecce Homo*: "One must avoid chance, outside excitation, as much as possible; walling oneself up, so to speak, is an act of instinctive elementary wisdom, a part of intellectual gestation. Shall I permit an alien thought to secretly scale that wall?" Further on, Nietzsche speaks in praise of impassive lethargy: "I see my future—a vast future—as a smooth sea: not a single wish disturbs the surface. Not for anything in the world would I want things to be different from what they are; as for me, I do not want to be different from what I am."

Through some mystery, I stripped myself of all desire at the very moment when I was winning the maximum of freedom. I feel lacustrine landscapes developing in my heart. I have awakened the old Chinese hermit within me.

JULY 8

In the evening, I build a fire on the shore and grill my fish there.

The evening is the dying of a dream. All the elements of a Romantic era reverie take their places before my front-row seat at around eight o'clock: still waters, swirls of mist, pastel-tinted eddies, birds skimming in low to their nests. Nature flirts with kitsch without ever falling into it.

Today, struck by Nietzsche's warning in *Ecce Homo*, I'm leaving the books alone: "I've seen this with my own eyes: gifted and rich natures 'inclined toward freedom' who have 'read themselves to death' by the time they are thirty, mere matches now, which must be struck to give off sparks—their 'thoughts.'" Compulsive reading relieves the anxiety that comes with tramping through the forest of meditation in search of clearings. Volume after volume, the reader settles for recognizing the expression of thoughts he was "working on" intuitively. Reading is reduced to either discovering the formulation of ideas that had been floating around in one's mind, or to the simple knitting together of connections among the works of hundreds of authors.

Nietzsche describes poor exhausted souls who can no longer manage to think unless they "look it up." Only the squeeze of lemon can awaken the oyster.

Hence the appeal of those people who see the world with eyes free of all reference, for whom memories of reading never come between them and the substance of things.

There was once a girl in my life who knew how to forget what she had read and who felt devotion for all forms of life. In southern France, we crossed the Camargue, the largest river delta in Western Europe. We rowed through the salt marshes, along canals, across lagoons. Flights of flamingoes sailed through the sunset. We camped out at night with hordes of mosquitoes that I would squash, bombarding them with chemicals. She said she loved them: "They bite, but to each his own, and besides, they keep men away from infested places so that the other animals can live there in peace." Twenty-two days ago, she left me.

My friends Thomas Goisque and Bernard Hermann arrive at twilight in Sergei's boat, and in the tradition of North Cedar Cape, we all get drunk on the beach, toasting lost loves and renewed friendships. Goisque is here on assignment for a magazine. Hermann has come to do what for decades has been the focus of his life as a Zen sage: the contemplation of shifting light on the skin of the world. He looks like a colonel in the Indian army: white cotton jacket, tortoiseshell glasses. His blond mustache and the "Pugachev's Rebellion" look

in his eye lead Russians to take him for a Don Cossack het-
man, but he informs them in a pidgin inherited from his jour-
neys through the Russia of Khrushchev and Brezhnev that
although he has Creole, Jewish, Celtic, Baltic, Hispanic, and
Teutonic genes, he can't think of a single Cossack ancestor.

JULY 9

Sergei left us a supply of seal fat yesterday. I paddle off southward with Goisque to leave the stinking substance on some
rocks in the hope of attracting a bear. From the table on my
beach, I can keep watch via binoculars. I spend my hours with
the promise of the bear.

My guests and I live together nicely. We fish, explore the
riparian forests, and discuss the subtle distinctions among
Russian nihilism, Buddhist acceptance, and peaceful Stoic
ataraxia. Sometimes Goisque and Hermann tackle their
memories of army life, at which point the conversation veers
between the moment when Shi poetry became Tang... and
the operations of the SDECE (France's external intelligence
agency from 1944 to 1982) when it was "militarized" into the
Eleventh Shock Parachutist Regiment.

JULY 10

The sky is more generous with its creatures than the forest.
No bear comes to the rendezvous with the smelly fat, which is
instead mobbed by barnacle geese, mergansers, tufted ducks,
and eiders. Two German kayakers arrive from the north at
nightfall. They set up camp on the cape beach, about a third of a
mile from the cabin, and come up to recharge their equipment

on my solar batteries. We have to look at their photos, their films, exchange e-mail addresses. When you meet someone nowadays, right after the handshake and a quick glance, you write down the website and blog information. Conversation has given way to a session in front of the screen. Afterward, you won't remember faces or tones of voice, but you'll have cards with scribbled numbers. Human society's dream has come true: we rub our antennae together like ants. One day we'll just take a sniff.

JULY 11

The German kayakers set out again in their perfectly organized crafts. At the same moment, four other oarsmen show up in my bay. These guys are not nearly as well equipped. Crappy gear: Russians. They're using garbage bags as watertight skirts for the hatch coamings. They're dressed like sailors, and they accept the three shots of rotgut the Teutons declined (on the grounds that it was too early in the day). Germans and Russians: the former would like to put the world in order, while the latter must endure chaos to demonstrate their genius.

The last visit of the day is worthy of the Balkan cinema of the '90s. From the north, heralded by cannon fire, a raft of planks floating on Ural truck wheel inner tubes comes drifting toward my shore. In the center of this floating island, enthroned on beams and braced by cables, sits a jalopy. Three Russians in full fatigue dress leap out onto the shingle: "Our raft is called the *Intrepid*!" They've got the mugs of killers, striped submariner middy blouses, and daggers in their belts. The car's universal joint has been pulled off its axis, tipped twenty degrees, and equipped with a propeller. On this *Kon Tiki* from hell, they are heading down to Irkutsk, taking turns piloting from the driver's seat. At the stern, a wood fire in an oil drum serves as a kitchen. When they leave, they fire off a small portable cannon, and I contemplate this raft, so much like life in Russia: an unwieldy, dangerous thing on the verge of shipwreck, a slave to the currents—but aboard which you can always make tea.

That evening, at the waterfall, while Hermann guards the home front, Goisque and I succeed in crossing the torrent above the falls. We reach the granite ridge where I'd found a good camping ledge during the winter. It takes us an hour to cover the last fifty yards of uneven terrain, defended by dwarf pines that catch our feet in their branches.

On the platform, I build a fire. The traverse is a lodge for a vigil of arms, one of those places where you make peace with yourself before a dawn execution. The kind of spot where—depending on your mood—you are flooded with either darkest despair or radiant joy. We smoke our Romeo no. 1 cigars; the night is calm, the moon already almost full. Why this desire to remake the world just when it's going out? Cumulus clouds obscuring the Buryat horizon ripen in the setting sun. The four elements play their parts. The water welcomes the shavings of lunar silver, the air is laden with fog, and the stones shimmer with banked heat. Why believe that God is anywhere else but in a sunset? The dogs have flopped down out under the pines. The fire burns higher; night falls. They meet.

Suddenly Aika darts down the slope with fangs bared while Bek huddles under the pines like an apartment dog lost out on the taiga. The little black watchdog barks in the darkness and we imagine a bear circling our camp.

JULY 12

Goisque, Hermann, and I are walking in silence on the beach at Middle Cedar Cape. In his *Life of Rancé*, Chateaubriand, crushed by modesty, remembers having walked along "under the weight of my mind."

At the tip of the cape, a moment of reflection at the cabin where that soul shipwrecked by the Red Century rotted away. Hermann: "A life without ever hearing a game-show host." In a clump of dwarf pines, on the shingle ridge that divides Baikal from the inland ponds, the dogs flush out a sitting duck, and we must restrain them from putting paid to the eggs. Aika still manages to gobble a little sparrow up alive, to the dismay of Hermann, who has been a strict vegetarian for forty years.

The six-o'clock sun has transformed the marsh into forest pools in an Arthurian wood. The mists of legends float across the water, parting at times to release a thousand darting diffractions in a scene tailor-made for a Victorian Gothic writer. In a fantasy novel of the late nineteenth century, dragonflies would become the winged steeds of fairies, the light flashing on the water would be the kisses of undines, the mist would be the breath of sylphs, and spiders would stand guard over the gates of the wind, while the still waters would shelter the cave of a tutelary god, and the rays of the setting sun, shooting grandly up over the mountain crests, would symbolize the golden road to the realms of Heaven. But we're mere men in a world of atoms and must get home before dark.

JULY 13

The Europeans have proceeded with the construction of third-generation pressurized water reactors, relaunched the Transgreen Project aiming to import solar energy produced in the Sahara, and there's a massive black tide offshore of Florida. I read these chronicles of human demiurgy in the newspapers Goisque brought with him.

Life in the cabin is a profession of faith in a form of energy that has nothing to do with man's age-old ambition to master the universe. The woodcutter's ax and the solar panel provide light and heat. Being frugal with energy is not a burden. Neither is the satisfaction of knowing one is self-sufficient, nor the spiritual comfort of enjoying the prodigality of the sun. Photovoltaic panels capture the photons showering down from the sky, and wood—which is fossilized solar light—releases its energy in fire.

Every calorie drawn from fishing or gathering, each photon assimilated by the body, is spent to fish, gather, draw water, and chop wood. The woodsman is an energy-recycling machine. Relying on the forest is a form of self-reliance. Without a car, the hermit walks. Without a supermarket, he fishes. Without a boiler, he chops wood. The principle of nondelegation concerns the mind as well: without a TV, he opens a book.

What do oil and uranium look like? What does the containment building of a pressurized water reactor contain? What is the composition of the crude oil flowing from the BP wellhead two and a half miles down? Who transforms these forces and brings them to us in the form of watts? Cabin communism means eliminating intermediaries. The hermit knows where his wood and water come from, along with the meat he eats, and the wild rose perfuming his table. The principle of proximity guides his life. He refuses to live in the abstraction of progress and draw upon an energy source about which he knows nothing. To be "modern" means refusing to worry about where the benefits of progress actually come from.

The other news in the paper concerns the corruption of the personnel of the French state, who sometimes betray a confounding clumsiness in hiding their malfeasance. Even the valets of the Marquis de Sade remembered to lock the doors of their master's boudoir. The ugliness of the men in suits and their impoverished command of the language are worse than their crimes.

JULY 14

The sun hoists the colors at four a.m., and I raise mine a little later. I've only three—sky, snow, blood—and the little flag snaps on the beach, flying from a fishing pole. For the fatherland on Bastille Day, Goisque, Hermann, and I down three times three vodka eye-openers. We salute the memory of Borodino, the bloodiest day of the French invasion of Russia—indeed, of all Napoléon's wars. I organize some "dancing in the streets" and teach Bek how to waltz. Aika, the bitch, refuses to dance. Is it legal to plant the French flag on the soil of Russia? Is it a provocation? I must remember to ask the next constitutional scholar who paddles by in a kayak.

JULY 15

Goisque and Hermann left this morning. Their friendly presence and the constant stream of rowers these past few days have screwed up my internal clock, and it will take me a few days to recover a rhythm based exclusively on the observation of the sun's progress around my clearing.

JULY 16

Cabin life is like sandpaper. It scours the soul, lays bare one's being, ensavages the mind, and reclaims the body for the wild, but deep in the heart it unfolds the most sensitive nerve endings. The hermit gains in gentleness what he loses in civility. "The less sensitive he was to suffering, perhaps, the more receptive our ancestor was to pleasure, and the more conscious of his happiness," writes Bachelard in *The Psychoanalysis of Fire*.

If he wishes to safeguard his mental health, an anchorite cast up on the shore must live in the moment. Let him begin to elaborate plans, and he will descend into madness. The present: a protective straitjacket against the sirens of the future.

The evening clouds put cotton nightcaps on the drowsy mountains.

Wild roses cluster at the feet of trees along the edge of the forest, turning their corollas toward their god, the Sun. I think of the description of the garden on the rue Plumet in *Les Misérables*. Jean Valjean has let it lie fallow, and Hugo makes a profession of pantheistic faith: "Everything toils at everything. . . . No thinker would dare maintain that the scent of the hawthorn is useless to the constellations. . . . Between beings and things, there are marvelous relations. . . ."

Taking Hugo's question even further: Who would claim that the fawn never dreams of tumbling surf, that the wind feels nothing when it strikes the wall, that dawn is unmoved by the trilling of titmice?

JULY 17

Figure it takes one day to split a supply of wood, catch four char, feed the dogs, repair the boards of a shed somewhat battered by a storm, and read *Typhoon*. Conrad's Captain MacWhirr is an anti-Ahab: he stands on the threshold of destiny, accepts the typhoon, does not seek to escape what is unavoidable. Why should we be moved by what is not of our own making? No white whale is worth getting worked up about. Carried to an extreme, indifference makes men seem obstinate, and Conrad's MacWhirr begins to seem a brute. The captain would make a good Russian hero. In Russia, to indicate that one doesn't give a damn, one says *mnye po figu*. And "pofigism" is a resigned indifference to all things. Russians boast of facing the convulsions of History, the challenges of the climate, and the villainy of their leaders with their own inner pofigism, which is not dependent on Stoic resignation or Buddhist detachment. Pofigism has no ambition to guide mankind to the virtue of Seneca or to hand out karmic merit badges. Russians ask simply that they be allowed to empty a bottle today because tomorrow will be worse than yesterday. Pofigism is a state of inner passivity corrected by a vital force. The deep contempt in which he holds all hope does not prevent the pofigist—whose event horizon is the end of the day—from snatching as much enjoyment as possible from the passing hours. MacWhirr, sweating on the bridge of his ship as he awaits the typhoon, might be one of the faithful in this Church of No Hope.

JULY 18

The fog surprises me as I'm cutting from cape to cape in the kayak. The sun manages to deploy its glories, edging breaks in the mist with spiky crowns like blindingly bright sea urchins. It's weather for being attacked by some Lake Baikal monster. I go ashore in front of the abandoned cabin and plunge into the forest toward the marshes, seeking wild onions, rhubarb, and bear's garlic. The mosquitoes mob me. I'd like to drag the people who write ads for mosquito repellant through here stark naked, so they'll tone down the bull on their labels. The ponds sparkle. The cedars darken the shores, and the wild roses brighten them. I return to the cabin laden with aromatic herbs. The lake is turning pink as clouds mottle the sky, now covered with lavender bruises and streaked with cyan blue. You'd need to be a forensic pathologist to fully appreciate a Baikalian sunset.

JULY 19

A shower on the beach. I'm washing with buckets of luke-warm water when Volodya arrives from Elohin in his little boat, bearing gifts of smoked fish. He has come to discuss a problem that enthralls Russians. "There are riots in your French cities! The Arabs are in revolt! Everything's going up in flames." My Russian vocabulary is too small for me to tell him properly that things are less serious but more complicated than that. And anyway, are they really? I'd have to explain that these movements are expressions of social anger and that the ethnic origins of the demonstrators may well impress the Russians, but are not stressed by French commentators. I'd have to show him that this is not a revolution. These public disturbances don't aim to overthrow bourgeois society but to break into it. Are these young people demanding liberty, power, and glory? Why are they burning cars in those pockets of poverty? To protest against the savaging of society by technology and the market? Or in despair at not owning the biggest and most beautiful cars themselves?

I remember my forays into such "sensitive" neighborhoods—an adjective applied to places marked by a certain odor of brutality. The little kids were quite lively and did me the honor of listening to what I had to say, but they made fun of my equipment, how I was dressed, and the way I talked. What I took away from such encounters was that they invest enormous tribal significance in clothing and conformist behavior, cultivate a sense of neighborhood loyalty, love expensive things, demonstrate an unhealthy obsession with appearance, believe that might makes right, show little curiosity about *the other*, and have their own linguistic codes: the distinctive signs of bourgeois society.

Ye gods of the woods—to live out here and insult these mountains by paying any attention to such things! As soon as Volodya takes off, I chase away such concerns and get back to my chores and my books.

JULY 20

Today I scale rugged terrain to 5,250 feet and clamber back down again: so much for the statistics. I'd decided to tackle the peak directly behind the cabin. First comes the long and difficult climb through the taiga. I get into the underbrush after 2,800 feet. The far edge of the forest marks the threshold of the upper world, where boulders torn from the summits have rolled all the way down to the ramparts of the trees. The silence is vast and still. The dogs pant in the heat. We drink straight from the cascading torrent. The canyon is growing tighter, giving Aika and Bek trouble with its rock steps and ledges. I sit down by clumps of mountain anemones to study the slow collapse of woods and scree slopes down to the lake-shore below.

It seems that some men check out women's hips to know if they will bear children easily. Others consider their eyes for signs that they will prove captivating lovers, or think the length of their fingers will reveal something about their sensuality. And some men study geography in the same ways.

These mountains offer nothing but a host of immediate sensations. Man will never improve on these ranges. Calculating souls will get nothing for their pains in this unpromising landscape wracked with grandeur, for it is unconquerable. Here nature relaxes for the sole appreciation of minds free from all ambition. The taiga is not a good playground for dreams of cultivation. Developers, buzz off back to Tuscany! Under temperate skies, there the land waits for man to mold it into countryside. Here, in this amphitheater, the elements reign for eternity. There were epic battles in volcanic periods, but now all is calm. The landscape: geology in repose.

At an elevation of 5,600 feet, I cut across scree slopes toward the peak. Up there, along the ridge dividing the basins of Lake Baikal and the Lena River, I have lunch with the dogs: three smoked fish and some wild onion. Another hour's march across dried lichens to the top at 6,890 feet, where the dogs and I nestle together for a nap. Until we're driven off by mosquitoes, the guardians of the summit, who defend it against all comers. Nature, in its genius, has deployed not armies of monstrous creatures, vulnerable to rifle fire, but tiny flying syringes whose buzzing drives one insane.

We beat a retreat down the northeastern versant and scramble down a scree slope, dislodging mini-avalanches with every step. I pass through a firn field—old snow not quite hardened yet into glacier ice—canted at a forty-degree angle, using two fine slabs of schist to cut out steps. The dogs howl before resigning themselves to going around the obstacle, and when the slope moderates, we start sinking into the snow. At 3,000 feet, confronted with a suspicious transverse fault, I instinctively leave the firn for its rocky edges, where a meltwater stream appears; the river beneath the snow makes a brief reappearance before vanishing into a gulf a hundred feet below.

JULY 21

Not one bird is singing. Not one ripple on the lake. Fog has swallowed up the world.

JULY 22

Their silent approach takes me by surprise: I become aware of their presence only when I hear the kayaks scraping over the shingle. Two colossi with shaved heads. They have bloodthirsty smiles but the gentlest of eyes. They're paddling to Olkhon Island at the rate of about thirty miles a day. They ask me for some tea, and while the kettle is coming to a boil, they announce that they are Shivaists and are traveling along the lakeshore to find sacred sites, for they consider Baikal to be the original birthplace of their god. The funny thing is that they look like Special Forces killers.

My ten years of education with the Brothers have left me enough residual patience to get through the spiritual mish-mash, liberally sprinkled with Sanskrit, that Sasha expounds to me for an hour, the gist of which is that Baikal's mountains are linked to sacred Mount Meru, that the Ural Mountains are a world hot spot for Celto-cosmic revelations, and that Zarathustra built the kurgans—those prehistoric burial mounds found in southern Russia and Ukraine—on the Indo-Sarmatian plains. I admire these believers who speak of such things with the same aplomb as if they'd just split a beer with God in the cabin next door. Since the collapse of the USSR, New Age theories have been the rage with Russians. After all, something had to fill the mystic vacuum left by the debunking of socialist dogma. Russians love esoteric explanations of the world and will never shrink from swallowing whole any of those theories that professional occultists would never dare even to mention in Western Europe. Russians aren't the sons of Rasputin for nothing.

It's a lovely idea, sailing around while trying to recognize in the shape of a landscape the physical transcription of a legend. This spiritual and symbolic distortion of geography takes one's breath away. Paddling along, my two friends detect signs, track correspondences. In a prominent hill they see a lingam; in the crenellation of a ridge, the trident of Shiva; and in a cabin, the "center of effort" where all forces are thought to concentrate.

After supper, Sasha and his disciple sit in the lotus position on the beach and recite a Hindu mantra. Sasha blows into his Tibetan conch shell. The bleating awakens Bek, who starts howling.

"My dog doesn't like the sound of the conch," I say.

Sasha gives me a strange look.

"Maybe he isn't a dog. . . ."

They tell me again that the North Cedar cabin is on an "energy knot" of great intensity. They head out southward. The blasts on the conch echo in the distance.

JULY 23

I'm paddling toward the Lednaya River. The lake smells like a dead body. The fog is back. The forest appears, withdraws, returns. At the river, I fish from the rocks, then dine on the product of my patience. Tonight my bivouac is the quintessence of campsites: lapping water, a meadow at the base of a cliff overlooking a calm lake, with a few birches to break up the breeze. The fish are roasting on the fire while the dogs wait for their share, and a moon the color of a delicate iced cookie is lounging among the clouds. I smoke a Partagás. Cigars are consecrated by the places where they are smoked: my memory is geographic. Cigars retain the atmosphere and genius of places even better than faces and conversations can.

The only thing missing this evening is the woman of my dreams.

JULY 24

Dawn, and the sound of an engine. It's Volodya, who has come to spread a net at the mouth of the Lednaya. I hail him from the top of the cliff. We talk for an hour, sharing tomatoes on the bow deck of the canoe. In his discussions of the *immediate*, the French philosopher and musicologist Vladimir

Jankélévitch speaks of that faculty the Russians have of spending long hours sitting at a table, clinging to the reefs of an island covered with abundance. Around the table awaits a hard, hostile world into which everyone must plunge, sooner or later, until a new table appears, a little farther on.

I head back, steering through the fog. The shoreline is my guide, like Ariadne's thread in the labyrinth. The storm has the last word, striking two hours after I get home.

JULY 25

I'm going to be saying good-bye to the dogs. I watch them sleeping, with their heads on the cabin doorstep. Why does everything finally happen? There's only one way to avoid the unavoidable.

JULY 26

"I'm leaving, and have barely passed the first of the elms that line the road. . . ." André Chénier, guillotined on July 25, 1794.

Sergei will come get me the day after tomorrow. We'll drop the dogs off at Elohin, where they'll stay until they find a master in a different cabin in the preserve.

I came here without knowing whether I'd find the strength to stay; I leave knowing that I will return. I've discovered that living within silence is rejuvenating. I learned two or three things that many people know without having to hole up somewhere. The virginity of time is a treasure. The parade of hours is busier than the plowing-through of miles. The eye never tires of splendor. The more one knows things, the more beautiful they become. I met two dogs, I fed them, and one day, they saved me. I spoke to the cedars, begged forgiveness from the char, and thought about my dear ones. I was free because without the *other*, freedom knows no bounds. I contemplated the poem of the mountains and drank tea while the lake turned pink. I killed the longing for the future. I breathed the breath of the forest and followed the arc of the moon. I struggled through the snow and forgot the struggle on the mountaintops. I admired the great age of trees, tamed titmice, and perceived the vanity of all that is not reverence for beauty. I took a look at the other shore. I knew weeks of silent snow. I loved to be warm in my hut while the tempest raged. I greeted the return of the sun and the wild ducks. I tore into the flesh of smoked fish and felt the fat of char eggs refresh my throat. A woman bade me farewell but butterflies alighted on me. I lived the most beautiful hours of my life until I received a message, and the saddest hours afterward. I watered the earth with tears. I wondered if one could become a Russian not through blood but through tears. I blew my nose on mosses. I drank liters of poison at 104° F, and I enjoyed pissing with a wide-screen view of Buryatia. I learned to sit at a window. I melted into my realm, smelled the scent of lichen, ate wild garlic, and shared trails with bears. I grew a beard, and time unfurled it. I left the cave of cities and lived for six months in the church of the taigas. Six months: a life.

It's good to know that out there, in a forest in the world, there is a cabin where something is possible, something fairly close to the sheer happiness of being alive.

JULY 27

A nap on the stones of the beach with the dogs draped on top of me. Aika and Bek, my masters in fatalism, my comforters, my friends who expect nothing more than what the *immediate* reserves for you in the dog dish of life, I'm truly fond of you.

Harsh sun, azure lake, wind in the cedars, ebb and flow of the waves: in my hammock, I think I'm on the coast of the Mediterranean. In the forest, I drink a last toast to life à la Crusoe. Spotting an anthill, I tap on it with my palm. The insects defend themselves, bombarding my hand with formic acid. My skin glistens with the fluid and I sniff it up into my sinuses when I down a shot of vodka. The effect of the ammoniated fumes is instant and stunning: the forest garbs itself in unheard-of colors.

I take apart the kayak, pack my bags. My life has unfolded here for months. I fold it back up. I've always lived in suitcases. My crates of provisions are empty. I eat some fish. It's over. Tomorrow, the return.

JULY 28

One last visit to the top of the hill to bid farewell to the lake. Here, I ask the genius loci to help me make peace with time. On our way downhill, Aika flushes a female eider, which beats the water with its right wing, pretending to be wounded. Bek is fooled and chases her into the water until he loses his footing.

Aika seeks the nest, finds it, and savages the six ducklings before I can intervene. I finish off the downy little things with a stone.

For a long time, the mother duck's mourning cries on the shore . . .

She grieves for the thousands of miles traveled for nothing; she grieves for her lost offspring. Life means holding on through the death of dear ones.

All it took was the instinctive snapping teeth of a little carnivore for an immense bright loneliness to descend on North Cedar Cape.

I'm sitting on the wooden bench waiting for Sergei's boat. The sun is beating down. The bags and trunks are piled up. The dogs are sleeping on the sand. And that mother duck weeping in the sunshine.

The morning has the taste of death, the taste of departure.

The dogs look up. A faint rumbling, confirmed: the boat. A dot grows larger and larger on the horizon. One last time.

ACKNOWLEDGMENTS

I express my gratitude and send greetings to the people who helped me throughout my stay in the cabin at North Cedar Cape.

Alexis Golovinov
Thomas Goisque
Cédric Gras
Bertrand de Miollis
Olivier Desvaux
Stéphanie Tesson
Bernard Hermann
Cyril Drouhet and Jean-Christophe Buisson of
    Figaro Magazine
François Fèvre
Florence Tran
Cyrille Benchimol
Georges Bonopéra
The Botravail team
Emmanuel Rimbert
Sylvie Granotier and Jean-Marie Rouart, for their reading
    suggestions
Les Équipements Millet and Patrice Folliet
And above all, Arnaud Humann

TRANSLATOR'S NOTES

1. Baikal is the deepest lake on earth and one of the most ancient in geological history. Much of Baikal's rich biodiversity is endemic to the lake, and at 85 percent of the total biomass of this "cauldron of evolution," *Epischura baikalensis* is the major zooplankton species there. In his book *Sacred Sea*, the environmentalist Peter Thomson describes not only how this janitorial service of scavenging copepods filters the world's largest and largely pristine freshwater lake with amazing efficiency, but also how modern industries on its shores have made Baikal a vat of pollution poisonous to its inhabitants. Besides the *Epischura*, in his Siberian journal Sylvain Tesson mentions in particular two more of the lake's unique creatures:

the omul, a whitefish species of the salmon family, and the Baikal seal, both of which have been listed as endangered. The *Epischura* ingest toxins, the fish eat the copepods, and the seals—among others—eat the fish. The "nasty irony" of the lake's famously clear waters, as Thomson says, is that if the *Epischura* die, so will Baikal.

2. The FSB has a long pedigree; here is a simplified genealogy. After the Russian Revolution swept away the secret police of Imperial Russia, Lenin created the Cheka, which in time became the GPU (part of the NKVD), and subsequently spun off to become the OGPU. The OGPU later moved back into the NKVD as the GUGB, moved out again into the NKGB, then back into the NKVD, finally separating out *again* into the NKGB only to wind up reassigned to the NKGB-MGB. Beria eventually combined the MGB and MVD into the MVD, but after Beria was purged, the MVD shed the secret police into the KGB. When the Soviet Union broke up in 1991, the KGB was dissolved and its functions distributed among the FSO, the SVR, and its main successor agency, the FSB, whose personnel are informally referred to in Russia as Chekists—which brings us full circle.

3. Around the third century AD, hermits and ascetics began moving into the Nitrian Desert of Egypt, and these growing desert communities of monks and nuns became known collectively as the Desert Fathers. Saint Anthony the Hermit (ca. 251–356), depicted in many a *Temptation of St. Anthony*, is the most famous exemplar of this movement, which greatly influenced the development of Christianity and provided the model for Christian monasticism.

4. The eighteenth-century adventurer Casanova's multivolume *Story of My Life* beggars description. The four allusions on this page refer to these stories:

Count Tiretta was Casanova's "companion in vice" and his guest, along with several women, at a gathering in a rented room overlooking the Place de la Grève in Paris to witness a man's execution there on March 28, 1757. Robert-François Damiens, who had attempted to assassinate Louis XV, was hideously tortured for four hours before his limbs were hacked off and his reportedly still-living torso burned at the stake. Damiens screamed so piteously that Casanova had to look away at one point—and noticed Tiretta quietly enjoying "indecent pleasures" from behind with one of the women guests, who never took her eyes off the entertainment in the square below.

On the run, a typical scenario, Casanova went to Parma, where he met a Frenchwoman he called Henriette, with whom he had a three-month affair and of whom he wrote with singular respect and admiration, perhaps because she declined, in the end, to "unite her destiny" with his. Many Casanova scholars consider Henriette to be his greatest love, the one who got away.

A castrato was a boy castrated before puberty to preserve his high singing voice, and the Italian castrato Bellino greatly impressed Casanova, whose experienced eye perceived that this singer was actually a lovely woman *en travesti*. In his memoirs Casanova calls her Teresa Lanti, and naturally, he had an affair with her. Bellino-Teresa subsequently had a son, Cesarino, who bore a remarkable resemblance to Casanova and whom she raised as her brother.

The story of Leonilda begins with Donna Lucrezia, a married woman with whom Casanova began an affair during a carriage ride to Rome. Casanova claims to have made love to both Lucrezia and her daughter, the seventeen-year-old virgin Angelica, in the same bed at the same assignation and only weeks before the daughter's wedding. Donna Lucrezia had a child by Casanova, Leonilda, who was raised as legitimate by her family—who were understandably aghast when Leonilda became engaged sixteen years later to...Casanova! The engagement was broken off, but Casanova claims to have repeated his mother-daughter coup by getting Donna Lucrezia and Leonilda into bed together, although he denied having sex with his daughter at that time. Years later, according to his memoirs, he encountered Leonilda again, now married to an impotent man, and this time he got her pregnant *with his own grandson*.

5. Perhaps the most famous example of "death by Baikal" occurred during the Great Siberian Ice March of the Russian Civil War. Pursued by the Red Army, Admiral Kolchak's White Russian troops retreated east in January and February of 1920 until their only way forward lay across the lake. Heading out in subzero temperatures made excruciating by the Arctic winds scouring the ice, around thirty thousand soldiers, their families, pack animals, carts, and possessions crossed to Transbaikal, but a great many people and animals froze to death along the way. For months the long trail of their corpses offered a macabre spectacle, until the spring thaw sent them and all the army's abandoned baggage to the bottom of Baikal.

6. Named after John Clipperton, an English pirate and privateer, Clipperton Island is an uninhabited and largely barren coral atoll of only 3.5 square miles in the eastern Pacific Ocean. In 1906 the British Pacific Island Company built a guano mining settlement there, installing one

Lieutenant Arnaud as governor of Clipperton and its colony of soldiers, their families, and sixty Italian workers. World War I and the Mexican Revolution made the resupplying of the island by ship impossible, but when a US Navy warship arrived to evacuate the island, Arnaud and some thirty colonists refused to leave. By 1917 scurvy and an ill-fated attempt to leave the island in a small boat had left only one man alive there, the lighthouse keeper, Victoriano Álvarez, who proclaimed himself King of Clipperton and began terrorizing the remaining women and children through rape and murder. When the USS *Yorktown* checked the atoll on July 18, 1917, they found the surviving women and children and the corpse of Álvarez, whom Arnaud's widow had killed in self-defense the day before with a hammer.

7. Vasily Grigorevich Perov (January 2, 1834–June 10, 1882) was one of the founding members of a group of Russian realist painters. His Wikipedia entry shows *The Hunters at Rest*, 1871.

8. Named for the Sarma River, which empties into the Small Sea Strait lying between Olkhon Island and the western shore of Baikal, this wind comes roaring out of its valley as if from a cannon and can reach hurricane force. Among the coldest and strongest of Baikal's winds, the *sarma* is only one of many specific air currents created by the mountain ranges of Baikal, and they vary according to geographical location, time of year, time of day, temperature, air pressure, etc. For added insight into the tremendous ecosystem of Lake Baikal, see the entertaining essay on these quirky and often quite dangerous winds—the *verkhovik, kultuk, kharakhaikha, gornaya* and others—at

www.magicbaikal.com/winds.php in the *Baikal Winds* section. Here, for example, is the description there of the *sarma*'s power: "Sarma can blow continuously for days and at times the wind is so strong that it can uproot trees, overturn boats, tear the roofs off houses and sweep cattle from the shores into the lake. The roofs of houses in the village of Sarma, situated in the valley of the river with the same name, are tied to the ground by the villagers."

9. Considered the greatest poet of the Six Dynasties Period (c. 220–589), Tao Yuanming (365–427) was the most famous of the Chinese "poets of reclusion," artists who retired to the countryside or wilderness to write, often in praise of the quiet life they found there. A noted recluse, Tao Yuanming was admired for the elegant way in which he extolled both the joys of leisure and the contentment of fulfilling one's duties, and beloved for the artless simplicity of the motifs that became emblematic of his style. A pastoralist who delighted in fields and gardens, he found solace from the hardships of a farmer's life in the cultivation of chrysanthemums, a flower that became his personal "seal" in later Chinese painting and literature, and his influence is still felt in modern English poetry.

10. Du Mu (803–852) was a prominent poet of the late Tang Dynasty, a golden age of Chinese poetry, but unlike Tao Yuanming, he cared deeply about statecraft and remained actively engaged in the Chinese bureaucracy all his adult life. Although he is appreciated for the bold, unconstrained energy of his long narrative poems, he is best known for his sensually descriptive quatrains.

11. While off in Irkutsk sorting out his visa problem, Tesson turned thirty-eight on April 26.

12. The nalim is a kind of burbot (a codlike fish) that is usu-
    ally eighteen to twenty inches long and weighs between
    eleven and fifteen pounds. This description from a Russian
    English-language website about native freshwater fishes
    says it all: "Large, widespread fish. A body extended,
    covered with very small scales with the big layer of slime.
    On either side of nostrils on a small short moustache, one
    more short moustache—on a chin. Colouring of a body
    from grey-black and dark-brown to brown with a reddish
    shade and the big stains or divorces. A belly light."